DOCTOR ZHIVAGO

A Critical Companion

DOCTOR ZHIVAGO

A Critical Companion

Edited by Edith W. Clowes

Northwestern University Press

The American Association of Teachers of Slavic
and East European Languages

Northwestern University Press

Evanston, Illinois 60208-4210

Copyright © 1995 by Northwestern University Press

Printed in the United States of America

ISBN 0-8101-1211-6

Library of Congress Cataloging-in-Publication Data

Clowes, Edith W.

Doctor Zhivago : a critical companion / edited by Edith W. Clowes.

p.   cm. — (Northwestern /AATSEEL critical companions to
Russian literature)

Includes bibliographical references.

ISBN 0-8101-1211-6

1. Pasternak, Boris Leonidovich, 1890–1960. Doktor Zhivago.

I. Title.   II. Series.

PG3476.P27D6795   1995

891.73'42—dc20   95-31482

                                                    CIP

Contents

Acknowledgments

The work of assembling this volume of critical materials on Boris Pasternak's *Doctor Zhivago* was aided by a number of people. Vera Proskurina, Elliott Mossman, and Evgeny Pasternak provided invaluable help at the outset. Jeannette Moss, Margaret Jackson Clowes, George L. Kline, Barry Scherr, and Jay West offered useful comments on the introduction. Carla Nelson and Marcia Smith typed the manuscript into the computer, and Carla Nelson helped compile bibliographical materials. Charlotte Moss completed a preliminary translation of Pasternak's correspondence conducted in Russian and of Boris Gasparov's and Dina Magomedova's articles. As always, the staff at Purdue's Interlibrary Loan Office did a great deal to procure source materials. To all these people I would like to express my thanks.

I am particularly grateful to the heirs of Boris Pasternak for the rights to translate the letters included in Part III.

The following essays were previously published, some in slightly different form, and appear here by permission: Carol J. Avins, "Yury Zhivago's Readers: Literary Reception in Pasternak's Novel and in His Time," in *Freedom and Responsibility in Russian Literature: Essays in Honor of Robert Louis Jackson*, edited by Elizabeth Cheresh Allen and Gary Saul Morson (Evanston, Ill.: Northwestern University Press and the Yale Center for International and Area Studies, 1995); Edith W. Clowes, "Characterization in *Doctor Zhivago*: Lara and Tonya," *Slavic and East European Journal* 3 (1990); Boris Gasparov, "Temporal Counterpoint as a Principle of Formation in *Doctor Zhivago*," a condensed translation of "Vremennoi kontrapunkt kak formoobrazuiushchii printsip romana Pasternaka 'Doktora Zhivago,'" in *Boris Pasternak and His Times: Selected Papers from the Second International Symposium on Pasternak* (Berkeley: Berkeley Slavic Specialties, 1989); Dina Magomedova, "The Relationship of Lyrical and Narrative

'Plot' in *Doctor Zhivago*," a condensed translation of "Sootnoshenie liricheskogo i povestvovatel'nogo siuzheta v tvorchestve Pasternaka," *Izvestiia Akademii Nauk SSSR: Seriia literatury i iazyka* 5 (1990).

Note on Transliteration

For ease of reading, the "y" system of transliteration (Thomas Shaw's System I) has been used in the text. In the bibliography the "i" system, or Shaw's System II, has been chosen for its greater accuracy.

I ✳ INTRODUCTION

Doctor Zhivago in the Post-Soviet Era: A Re-Introduction

EDITH W. CLOWES

Contemporary Soviet literature, it seems to me, stands apart from its predecessors in that its existence is assured no matter whether people read it or not.
—Letter to N. Aseev, February 1953

I need to do something dear to me and my very own, riskier than usual, I need to break through to the public.
—Letter to S. N. Durylin, June 1945

Art, artistic creation (realism) is obsession with actuality (reality), it is the beautiful suffering of people who must transfigure outer forms. To be an artist, in my view, means to be obsessed by the idea of life and the gathering of experience. Real art is what transfigures the simple things of everyday into a fairytale. Art without the presence of the Holy Spirit, genius or philosophical substance, that is, without its elemental, eternal, and necessary gifts, does not exist for me.
—Interview with Italian newspaper, Visto

The Reception of *Doctor Zhivago*

In the last century few works of art have created such a firestorm as Boris Pasternak's *Doctor Zhivago* (written 1946–55). In recent years the only comparable (and even *more* desperate) case has been Salman Rushdie's *Satanic Verses*. Having censured *Doctor Zhivago* in the Soviet Union in 1956, the Soviet authorities then tried to prevent Pasternak's work from being published in the West.

Despite everything, the renegade Italian communist Giangiacomo Feltrinelli carried through and produced it in Italian translation in 1957. The publication of the original Russian text and numerous other translations followed immediately. The real furor started in October 1958, when Pasternak was awarded the Nobel Prize in literature, an award given to recognize lifelong literary achievement.

The Soviet establishment insisted that the prize was really in recognition of the undeserving *Doctor Zhivago*, a book perceived as unpatriotic and anti-Soviet in the extreme. The Soviet apparat had long coveted the Nobel Prize for their own literary lion, Mikhail Sholokhov, the author of *And Quiet Flows the Don* (*Tikhii don*). The fact that Sholokhov was overlooked was then interpreted as a sign that the prize was actually a weapon in the cold war arsenal, an attack by the capitalist West on the grand project of building communism. The Soviet literary and political press followed the announcement of October 23 with a barrage of hostile "reviews" and resolutions. On October 25 the editors of *Novyi mir* published a lengthy report (actually written two years before) explaining that they could not publish something so "deeply unfair," "historically slanted," "deeply anti-democratic" (Bakhnov and Voronin, 41). On October 26, *Pravda* dismissed *Doctor Zhivago* as "literary trash" and a "malicious lampoon of the socialist revolution" (Bakhnov and Voronin, 44). Galina Nikolaeva, a minor critic, called Pasternak's novel "spit on our Soviet people" (Bakhnov and Voronin, 93). Within the week the Moscow branch of the Writers' Union had dubbed Pasternak a traitor, and Pasternak had been expelled from the Writers' Union – an act of blacklisting that meant the writer would be completely isolated, would henceforth get no contracts, and that all the perquisites of privilege (the best hospital care, food, even his dacha) could be denied him. The next blow was an article by the critic V. E. Semichastnyi, ghost-edited by Khrushchev himself, calling Pasternak "worse than a pig" because "a pig never befouls where it eats or sleeps" (Bakhnov and Voronin, 115). Pasternak's deportation from the Soviet Union was averted only by a personal petition to Khrushchev and by Pasternak's subsequent refusal of the Nobel Prize.

The object of all this fuss was a long narrative about a doctor-poet who lives through the Bolshevik revolution of 1917 and the ensuing civil war. Doctor Zhivago is primarily an observer devoted to hearing the higher revolutionary "music" of the age, but openly critical of Bolshevik movers and shakers hubristic enough to claim for themselves the role of history's enforcers. He is equally critical of their often malicious followers. What particularly piqued the rage of the Soviet literary establishment was that Pasternak fully ignored the ideological requirements of Soviet command literature, socialist realism. In *Doctor Zhivago* there is neither "positive hero" nor party presence. The concept of "the people" or nationality, a central ingredient in the socialist realist recipe, is treated in negative terms. "Revolutionary reality" is most ambiguously conveyed, certainly not leading inevitably to a bright future.

All the sound and fury of the official response drowned out the underground dialogue that went on between Pasternak and his readers who saw *Doctor Zhivago* in manuscript form. Pasternak's book was an answer to a lifelong dream to produce a long prose work about his generation and its historical fate. For much of his career a quite esoteric poet close to the avant-garde, Pasternak now wanted to write "simply" and in a way that would be accessible to a broad readership. He felt guilty that he had been spared while so many of the great poets and artists of his generation had perished: the poets Vladimir Mayakovsky and Marina Tsvetaeva had committed suicide, the writer Boris Pilnyak and the theater director Vsevolod Meyerhold had been arrested and shot, and the actress Zinaida Raikh, Meyerhold's wife, had been murdered. As he wrote in the late 1940s to his cousin Olga Freidenberg, a classicist at Leningrad University: "I am guilty before everyone. But what can I do? So here is the novel – it is a part of this debt, proof that at least I *tried*" (Pasternak to Olga Freidenberg, letter of November 30, 1948; texts of all letters quoted in this Introduction are given in Part III) – that is, tried to bear witness to the unspeakable suffering of so many people at the hands of a tyrant shielding himself with a grandiose idea.

Pasternak decided finally that he had to write in a way that would certainly be anathema to the Stalinist literary apparatus, the editors, critics, and censors who were bent on controlling access of writers to real readers, who insisted on their own ideological idiom or, as Pasternak put it, their "idiotic clichés." He knew that his work was "not destined for the contemporary press." In 1945, just as he was getting started during the euphoria and the high hopes for freer times following the victory of World War II, he wrote: "I need to do something dear to me and my very own, riskier than usual, I need to break through to the public" (Borisov and Pasternak, "Materialy," 221). And, finally, Pasternak wanted this work to be a philosophical statement and a statement of faith, of his "views on art, the Gospels, human life in history and many other things." "The atmosphere of this thing," he wrote, "will be my own Christianity" (Pasternak to Olga Freidenberg, letter of October 13, 1946). And this insistence on a private religious vision, he knew, would be perceived as a direct challenge to the "scientific" atheism of the Stalinist state. As he wrote to Nina Tabidze, the widow of the well-known Georgian poet Titsian Tabidze (arrested and shot as an "enemy of the people" in the late 1930s), Pasternak felt that with this novel he had finally been able to see things clearly, to tell the truth: "Everything is untangled, everything is named, simple, transparent, sad. Once again, afresh, in a new way, the most precious and important things, the earth and the sky, great warm feeling, the spirit of creation, life and death, have been delineated" (Borisov and Pasternak, 244). And, as he told the sculptor Zoya Maslenikova, *Doctor Zhivago* could be seen as "anti-Soviet" only if "by Soviet one is to understand the desire not to see life as it is" (Maslenikova, 21).

Pasternak's efforts to tell the truth, *his* truth, was indeed morally and spiritually uplifting for many of his unofficial readers, as well. When Pasternak asked his cousin Olga Freidenberg to give her judgment of his novel, she answered passionately, "What do I think of it? I am at a loss: what do I think of life? This is life in its broadest and greatest sense." And somewhat further on: "It is a special version of the Book of Genesis." And at the end of her letter: "But what I'm writing isn't what I perceive. Instead of answering with a letter I should really answer with a long kiss. How I understand you in what is most important to you!" (November 29, 1948). Ariadna Efron, the daughter of the great poet Marina Tsvetaeva, wrote a long, detailed, very critical and very passionate letter to Pasternak. She concluded it with the following apotheosis, implying that Pasternak, like God, had re-created the world: "How good it is that you have done what only you could do. You didn't let them all [the intellectuals and artists squandered by the Soviet state] slip away nameless and un-identified, you collected them all in your own good and intelligent hands and you brought them to life with your breath and your labor. You have become stronger and stricter, clearer and wiser. Thank you" (November 28, 1948). The writer Varlam Shalamov, now fa-mous for his stories about the Stalinist labor camps, wrote Pasternak a number of thoughtful letters about *Doctor Zhivago*. In 1956 he expressed his gratitude to the beleaguered poet: "Let me tell you again, probably for the thousandth time, . . . that I am proud of you, I believe in you, I idolize you. . . . I never wrote you this, but it has always seemed to me that you are the conscience of our age." And further: "You are the honor of our time, you are its pride. In the future our time will be justified by the fact that you lived in it" (August 11, 1956). What is more, Shalamov promised Pasternak what he had yearned for and what he would not receive in his life-time: access to the mass reader. He had written earlier, in 1954: "I do not know how official critics will like the novel. The reader who has not yet been weaned from genuine literature is waiting for just this sort of novel. And for me, an ordinary reader who has long yearned for genuine books, this novel will remain a great event for a long, long time" (January 1954).

It is a pleasure to reintroduce *Doctor Zhivago* to a generation of readers that is living in a world without the cold war and without the Soviet brand of totalitarianism (but with a multitude of smaller dic-tatorships and ethnic and civil wars that have replaced the single big one), and without the polarized cultural and political context that initially contributed to the success of *Doctor Zhivago*. Certainly it is crucial to recognize the extreme historical significance of *Doctor*

Zhivago and the role of the Pasternak affair in creating an underground culture in Russia, that support network for intellectuals and writers critical of the system. It is equally important to understand that this novel initiated the system of literary production known as *samizdat* (literally "self-publishing") and *tamizdat* (publishing beyond the boundaries of the Soviet Union).

The different view of the Russian civil war that *Doctor Zhivago* offered, implicating the old Bolsheviks and Lenin in the murderous insanity of Stalinism, represented a total rejection of the Soviet official version of the two revolutions of 1917 and the civil war (1918–21). As Pasternak remarked to the sculptor Zoya Maslenikova in 1958, "in *Doctor Zhivago* the revolution is not treated as a cake with cream. For some reason people normally treat it as a cake with cream. I am criticized for ignoring the established views of these historical events and thus I have allegedly violated what has been interpreted somehow by someone as the interests of the state. That is like standing on the shore, shouting to a ship that is pulling away from the pier bound for an ocean voyage that one has forgotten a small piece of baggage" (Maslenikova, 18). Pasternak was clearly bound on such an "ocean voyage," taking the huge risk of a long view of a history, a view that deliberately ignored the traditional hyperbolic formulas and black-and-white judgments of ritualized Soviet historiography.

What is more, as the well-known critic Andrei Sinyavsky has suggested, *Doctor Zhivago* was written in the guise of a historical novel but is really a novel for and about the future. It challenges an attitude toward history well expressed by O'Brien, the evil genius of George Orwell's dystopian novel, *1984*, that whoever controls the past certainly controls the future. By bearing witness in his own way to the experience of his own generation, Pasternak wrested historical and literary truth from the hands of establishment editors, critics, and censors. All this is certainly enough to assure Pasternak's novel, finally published in Russia in 1988 in huge editions, a special position in the post-Soviet literary canon. And, indeed, *Doctor Zhivago* is now required reading for high school students bound for university.[1] For

Russian readers *Doctor Zhivago* deals with a painful historical reality that will long be with them.

The situation is somewhat different for the English-speaking public for which the book – and David Lean's 1965 movie – are no longer new. Whether or not *Doctor Zhivago* continues to be popular depends in part on the following consideration: Are the central issues and artistry of this work sufficient to elevate it above its specific historical context and offer something to later generations of readers who are not versed in the details of the Russian Revolution? What follows is a discussion of *Doctor Zhivago* in the context of Pasternak's other major works and a delineation of a number of problems central to the novel's structure and meaning.

The Place of *Doctor Zhivago* in Pasternak's Art

Until he wrote *Doctor Zhivago*, Pasternak was primarily known as a poet, albeit a poet who had also written short stories and longer autobiographical prose. Born in 1890, he came of age in an era dominated by poetry. The novel as an innovative literary form was generally perceived to have been exhausted by two of the world's greatest novelists: Dostoevsky, who had died in 1881, and Tolstoy, who was alive until 1910 and was an acquaintance of the Pasternak family. Still, from his earliest years as a poet, Pasternak yearned to write long prose, preferably a novel, and one about the revolution. It is one of the distinctive facts of Pasternak's creative life that for the length and breadth of his career of forty-odd years he dreamed of and planned to write a novel, only to complete one in 1955. The five ensuing years before his death in 1960 were taken up with the scandal caused by this masterpiece. Another key feature of Pasternak's writing was the idiosyncratic interrelationship of prose and lyricism in all his work. Throughout his life, Pasternak insisted that poetry was "easier" to write than prose and somehow preparatory to it. In his autobiographical work, *Safe Conduct* (1931), he admitted that for much of his early life he dismissed poetry writing as mere "versifying experiments" and added that it was an "unfortunate weakness."[2]

Time and again he repeated the thought that "a poem is to prose as a sketch is to a painting. Poetry seems to me one big sketchbook" (E. Pasternak, *Boris Pasternak*, 590). Importantly, Pasternak believed that verse did not have the weight and muscle to bear historical and philosophical material (Borisov and Pasternak, "Materialy," 207).

Despite this tendency on Pasternak's part to dismiss poetry as too easy and to glorify prose as difficult, the two modes of writing actually share a very close relationship in his work, no matter what the genre. Pasternak remarked on the interaction between the two in *Safe Conduct*: "we drag everyday things into prose for the sake of poetry. We draw prose into poetry for the sake of music. This, then, I called art, in the widest sense of the word."[3] Indeed, one of the hallmarks of Pasternak's poetry is its "prosiness," that is, its captivating mixture of language from everyday life – colloquialisms, images of the ordinary, even the banal – with elevated, one might even say sublime, imagery. What is more, if we tend to associate narrative form with prose, then Pasternak's poetry can seem "prosy" in that it often implies or openly tells a story. Much in the tradition of the greatest Russian poet of the early twentieth century, Aleksandr Blok, Pasternak wrote poems in clusters or cycles unified by a single narrative line. He also wrote long narrative poems. It is equally true that lyric features dominate his prose works, even *Doctor Zhivago*. In addition to strong use of alliteration, paranomasia, metonymy, and the like, we typically find an amorphous plot, vague characterization, or what Lazar Fleishman has called "embryonic personalities" – the predominance of description over action. Perhaps most important is the symbolic – even mythic – character of the narrative as a whole, that is, an emphasis on the story not so much as an "imitation" or reproduction of sense experience but as a kind of "sacrament," a symbol of something hidden (Fleishman, *Boris Pasternak*, 42–43).

Another feature of Pasternak's prose style needs to be mentioned, the specifically philosophical discourse that represents a third mode of writing, or "discourse," together with the lyrical and the prosaic. Long sections, primarily in Pasternak's autobiographical prose, *Safe Conduct*, *People and Situations*, *I Remember*, and *Doctor Zhivago*, are characterized by a single voice in monologue, offering a rational, synthetic interpretation of those "hidden" or mysterious aspects of being, experience, and knowledge that can be articulated in lyric or narrative form, but perhaps not made fully conscious. Such meditations may be on human nature, time, or existence, but are particularly directed at articulating an aesthetic – almost as a kind of armor against academic philosophers, political demagogues, and, in particular, those ideologically committed critics who are inclined to harness art to serve their own purposes. True to his modernist nature, Pasternak defends and elevates his art by building into it its own rhetorical armor.

In assuming a position on the interface between poetry and prose, Pasternak was consciously throwing a backward glance at Russia's first great national poet, Aleksandr Pushkin, who, a century earlier, had made the transition from verse to prose that was an essential step in the formation of the standard Russian literary language. If in the 1920s Pasternak came to believe that only prose would have the power to cope with historical breadth and philosophical depth, then Pushkin in the 1820s had written that "erudition, politics and philosophy have not yet explained themselves in Russian; we have absolutely no metaphysical language. Our prose is so badly refined that even in simple correspondence we are obliged to *create* idioms to explain the most ordinary concepts."[4] More than ever, the Pushkin of the transitional period became an important model for Pasternak as he wrote *Doctor Zhivago*. Pasternak called his novel a "novel in prose" in conscious, clear distinction to his predecessor whose famous novel *Evgeny Onegin* (1823–31) was subtitled a "novel in verse" (letter to Freidenberg, October 5, 1946). It is not by chance that *Evgeny Onegin* is read and reread by Yury, Tonya, and her father as they while away the winter of 1918–19 in the Varykino idyll (part 9). Neither is it by chance that Pushkin's lengthiest prose fiction, the historical romance *The Captain's Daughter* (*Kapitanskaia dochka*, 1833–36) finds frequent echo in the second half of *Doctor Zhivago* (Smirnov, 130–31). These two works form the major milestones in Pushkin's own effort to shift from long verse narrative to the prose novel.

It is certainly a mistake to interpret Pasternak's long literary career as preparation for the single work that he saw as its crowning achievement. Such earlier works as the poetry cycle, *My Sister – Life*, and the autobiographical prose *Safe Conduct* stand on their own among the crown jewels of twentieth-century Russian literature. Still, what emerged as *Doctor Zhivago* stands in a very close relationship to earlier works – in theme, style, and in choice of autobiographical and historical material. *Doctor Zhivago* recapitulates many aspects of Pasternak's first big public, literary success, the poetic cycle, *My Sister – Life* (written 1918–19, published 1922). Both convey the elation of the summer of 1917 (B. Pasternak, 5:6–8) after the first, February Revolution had happened "as if by mistake" and everyone felt suddenly free. At the heart of both works is the experience of being in love. Both works celebrate the tremendous feminine life force of nature (Harris, 395). What Pasternak wrote then about *My Sister – Life* would certainly apply to *Doctor Zhivago*: that both reflect the character of revolution at the moment "when it returns humans to human nature and views the state through the eyes of natural law" (E. Pasternak, *Boris Pasternak*, 298).

In the early 1920s Pasternak formulated the goal of writing a long narrative in prose. In a poem written shortly after *My Sister – Life*, he bids farewell to poetry: "I will say so long to verse, my mania – I have an appointment with you in a novel" (E. Pasternak, *Boris Pasternak*, 316). And here Pasternak once again makes clear that for him prose and poetry do not occupy opposite spheres. Abandoning the verse *form*, Pasternak kept his "appointment" with lyric *discourse* by experimenting in the new and, for him, difficult form of the novel.

Pasternak's first major piece of prose fiction was the novella *The Childhood of Louvers* (*Detstvo Liuvers*, 1922). He wanted this piece to be the first part of a novel about the coming-into-consciousness of a young girl, Zhenia Louvers, the daughter of a Belgian factory director in the Urals. Although Zhenia Louvers has typically been viewed by critics as a prototype of the heroine of *Doctor Zhivago*, Lara Guichard, it would be more accurate to say that both characters are evidence at once of Pasternak's feminine vision of human consciousness and his lifelong sensitivity to the social condition of women. As the author's son, Evgeny Pasternak, has pointed out, the last names of both characters remind us of this concern: A "louver" in English is a grilled ventilating window in a turret or an attic, while the French word "guichet" is a grille over a window (E. Pasternak, *Boris Pasternak*, 497). Both characters are vehicles for what Pasternak implied was a "feminine" aesthetic of receptivity, perception, and meditation (this is opposed in *Safe Conduct* to the theatrical aesthetic of Mayakovsky with his foregrounding and dramatization of the [male] poet's egocentric persona). In Zhenia and in his first introduction of Lara in part 2 of *Doctor Zhivago*, Pasternak focuses on the relationships between sense *per*ception and rational *con*ception and between language – the ability to name things – and consciousness.

In the mid-1920s Pasternak's interest in historical themes bore fruit. Just as the summer of 1917 had been a moment of ecstasy in Pasternak's life, so 1905 was a key year in Pasternak's personal myth of coming of age. With the twentieth anniversary of the uprisings of 1905, Pasternak produced two long narrative poems, "1905," an attempted epic, but really a rapturous recounting of events in the poet's own life; and "Lieutenant Shmidt," about a naval officer, Petr Shmidt, who led a mutiny in 1905 in the Black Sea Fleet. The year 1905 would mark an important high point in part 2 of *Doctor Zhivago*, showing Lara's perception of the December revolt in Moscow's Presnia neighborhood. Here she takes delight in the "honest boys," the rebels whose shooting seems for a moment to liberate her from her emotional enslavement to Komarovsky (2:18–19; citations are taken from *Doktor Zhivago* in *Sobranie sochinenii v 5–i tomakh*, vol. 3 [Moscow: Khudozhestvennaia literatura, 1990]. The part and chapter numbers are given in parentheses in the text).

Pasternak's first completed effort at novel writing came with *Spektorsky*, which, in imitation of Pushkin's *Evgeny Onegin*, he subtitled a "novel in verse." He wrote *Spektorsky* (1931) over five years from 1925 to 1929 and with a good deal of difficulty. Here again Pasternak showed a strong interest in history and the interaction between the macrohistory of societies and nations, and the microhistory of personal experience. This was Pasternak's first sustained effort to create a fictional hero in the context of a novel. It is significant that some of his qualities resurface in Yury Zhivago. Pasternak calls Sergei Spektorsky a "person without merits" [*chelovek bez zaslug*].[5] Spektorsky is what has been called a "metonymous hero," that is, a personality without a clear center, without a will, not a deliberate active agent – a kind of "man without qualities," to borrow Robert Musil's term (Aucouturier, 43). As with Zhenia Louvers and later Yury Zhivago, Spektorsky is both passive and perceptive.

The limits of verse became obvious to Pasternak as he worked on *Spektorsky*. He wanted to depict war and revolution in the second part of his novel but he decided against this plan because, as he put it, "verse cannot deal with the characterizations and formulations most needed and logical for this part" (Borisov and Pasternak, "Materialy," 207). Once again the material of history was beyond the powers of poetic form. And again Pasternak felt the pressing need to turn to prose. His next major work was indeed in prose, his autobiography, *Safe Conduct* (1931). Here Pasternak gave a quite mannered account of his early life, his travels, and his personal relationships. Based on this autobiographical narrative structure, Pasternak gave full rein to meditations on philosophy, the nature of language, and the relationship between political power and art. *Safe Conduct* and *Doctor Zhivago* stand in close spiritual relation to one another. Each has been called a "book of thoughts" (*kniga myslei*) (Sinyavsky, 361). Pasternak noted aptly that the philosophical world of *Doctor Zhivago* is really "the world of *Safe Conduct* only without theorizing, in the form of a novel, broader and more mysterious" (Borisov and Pasternak, "Materialy," 223). Certainly the two are very close, sharing expressed perceptions of Christianity, the Bible and its links to literary-cultural tradition. In the earlier work, Pasternak called the Bible the "notebook of humanity" and continued: "[the Bible] is vital not when it is required, but when it is responsive to all the comparisons with which the ages receding from it gaze back at it."[6] What is theorized in *Safe Conduct* is put into practice in *Doctor Zhivago*.[7]

The decade of the 1930s was filled with frustration for Pasternak: he warmed to the task of writing a novel just as external circumstances kept him from working on this project. At first, he was hampered by financial need and later by isolation, depression, and fear. In 1933 Pasternak mentioned to the godfather of Soviet letters, Maksim Gorky, that he needed to write short works and publish quickly in order to support his family, which through a divorce and remarriage had suddenly doubled in size (Borisov and Pasternak, "Materialy," 209). During the early 1930s, as the politics of "command literature," or writing in praise of Stalin's grandiose (and, in Pasternak's view, awful and dehumanizing) agricultural and industrial projects, stifled other possibilities for literary expression. Pasternak resorted to translating for a living. And in addition to everything else, he experienced what he called a crisis of readership. No longer willing to write relatively esoteric poetry and prose, he was all the more unwilling to write for the "intrusive" reader – the apparatus of control dominated by editors, critics, and censors, and, indeed, Stalin himself. As he wrote to the novelist Lydia Chukovskaya in 1938, he did not know for whom he would write a novel, because he felt so isolated from a natural audience (Borisov and Pasternak, "Materialy," 215). As Carol J. Avins shows in her essay here, this concern with defining a readership in the heavily controlled circumstances of Stalinist culture would become an important theme in *Doctor Zhivago*.

During the middle of the decade Pasternak devoted his spare time to a project subsequently known as "Patrick's Notes" (Fleishman, "Ot 'Zapisok Patrika'"). This was going to be an autobiographical novel told by one Patrick Zhivul't about the years of war and revolution – really, much the same old project but with a more restrained, modest, and accessible style. As Pasternak wrote in October 1934, to his cousin Olga Freidenberg: "I'd like finally for the first time to write something worthy, humane, in prose – grayly, boringly, and modestly – something big, nourishing. But I have no time."[8] Now Pasternak drew on the example of a new and unexpected model, Anton Chekhov, who wrote modest, simple prose and remained committed to the highest ideals (Borisov and Pasternak, "Materialy," 210).

"Patrick's Notes," published in 1937–39, does not stand on its own as an artistic work and may truly be viewed as a prototype for *Doctor Zhivago*. Most obviously, the surnames of both heroes, Zhivul't and Zhivago, have *zhiv-* or "life," "living," "alive," at their root. Both heroes are orphans, raised by the Gromekos, who have a daughter named Tonya. The heroine, Evgeniya Istomina, the mature Zhenya Louvers, is from the Urals, as Lara Guichard is. Istomina's husband is a physics and mathematics teacher in a city called Yuryatin; Lara's husband, Pasha Antipov, is a classics and history teacher who teaches himself math and physics and then starts to teach those subjects, as well, to other people. Both Istomina and Lara Guichard/Antipova have a daughter named Katya. Finally, both works deal with historical and social themes associated with the unrest of 1905, the revolutionary year 1917, and the civil war (1918–21).

During the years of the Great Terror (1936–38) during which much of the Old Bolshevik elite, generals, writers, and artists perished, Pasternak retreated increasingly into silence, sure that he would not have to wait long for the late-night knock at his door. In 1939, the great theater director Vsevolod Meyerhold invited Pasternak to translate Shakespeare's *Hamlet*, and soon after, both Meyerhold and his wife, Zinaida Raikh, perished at the hands of the security police. Pasternak persisted in his translation, finding in it the mental space to escape constant fear (Borisov and Pasternak, "Materialy," 219).

Hamlet suggested a heroic type that was close to Pasternak's heart (Fleishman, *Boris Pasternak*, 220). In Pasternak's great translation/interpretation of Shakespeare's play Hamlet became a Christ figure, passively but courageously resisting political evil, sacrificing himself for the truth, highly conscious, perceptive, and able to name things by their true names. In the years after Stalin's death, Pasternak's *Hamlet* became an archetype for the dissident intelligentsia in its resistance to the Soviet apparat. But for Pasternak in the early 1940s it offered a heroic character that was eventually reincarnated in Yury

Zhivago. As the first poem in the cycle of the Zhivago poems makes evident, Zhivago himself was fully aware of shaping his own fate after that of Hamlet.

Hard to believe as it may be, the years of suffering and deprivation during World War II were welcomed by many, including Pasternak, as a relief after the insane terror and treachery of the late 1930s. As one character in *Doctor Zhivago* puts it: "When the war broke out, its real horrors, its real danger and threat of real death were a blessing compared to the inhuman reign of fictions, and they brought relief because they limited the magic power of the dead letter."[9] Most important for the creative history of *Doctor Zhivago*, Pasternak broke free of his isolation and forged an image of the reader for whom he would write. He felt jubilant at being involved with a general national effort to save the country from invaders. Opportunities for publishing opened up again, and it became possible to give readings to audiences that were not composed solely of party hacks. In her memoirs Nina Muravina gives an inspired description of one such meeting with Moscow University students. It was a great breakthrough to discover an audience hungry for his art. What is more, during 1945 and 1946 Pasternak learned that he had foreign admirers, particularly among a group of English "personalists," who preached the "politics of the unpolitical" and viewed Pasternak as a great survivor of Soviet communism and a true hero (Fleishman, *Boris Pasternak*, 259). This too was an audience for whom he wanted to write.

Soon after, these hopes were dashed when late in 1946 the apparat renewed its attacks on writers, this time on the poet Anna Akhmatova and the satirist Mikhail Zoshchenko. Pasternak realized that Soviet society was not going to become freer, and he set to work, quietly determined to realize his dream of writing a novel. He saw it as his parting shot; as he wrote to his cousin Olga Freidenberg, he wanted "to give a historical image of Russia over the last forty-five years and, at the same time, in all aspects of its plot – difficult, sad, and worked out in detail, as ideally with Dickens or Dostoevsky" (October 13, 1946).

It is important to note that, as before, Pasternak was obliged to translate literary works to support this project that, under existing political conditions, would bring him no income at all. He translated the whole of Goethe's *Faust*, 1 and 2, a work that gave him at least as much of a sense of spiritual freedom as *Hamlet* had earlier. As he said to Maslenikova, translating *Faust* "helped me to become bolder, freer, to break bonds of some sort, not just of political and moral prejudice, but in the sense of form" (Maslenikova, 107; see also Livingstone, "Pasternak and Faust").

In concluding our discussion of the place of *Doctor Zhivago* in Pasternak's oeuvre, it will be helpful to provide a schematic chronology of the composition of the novel itself:[10]

Winter 1945–46	working title is *Boys and Girls*; parts 1 and 2
August 1946	starts part 3
Fall 1946	meets Olga Ivinskaya at offices of *Novyi mir*; Ivinskaya becomes a living archetype for Lara
November–December 1946	reworks part 2 extensively; first three poems complete: "Hamlet," "Indian Summer," "Winter Night"
January 1947	signed contract with *Novyi mir* for a novel entitled *Innokenty Dudorov*. The contract was later annulled.
April 1947	Part 3 finished. Attacks in press against Pasternak
Spring 1948	Part 4
April 1948	10 poems for the novel completed
April–May 1948	reworks parts 3 and 4

1948	*Doctor Zhivago* becomes lasting title
July 14, 1948	Book 1 typed in form that Feltrinelli published. Later corrected by Pasternak
October 1949	Ivinskaya arrested
December 1949	Part 5
October 1950	Part 6
1951–52	Part 7 finished May 1952; October 1952 – heart attack
February 1953	Part 8 finished
March 5, 1953	death of Stalin
Summer 1953	11 poems written, 2 deleted in final revision, part 17 nearly complete, parts 9–14 drafted by November 1953
Fall 1953	Ivinskaya released
December 10, 1955	final draft of novel completed
1957	published in Milan by G. Feltrinelli

Of particular interest in this chronology is Pasternak's tremendous burst of creative energy following his own heart attack and the death of Stalin. Having spent almost eight years writing the first half of the novel, he drafted the whole second half (ten parts) in a scant twelve months and completed the final draft of the whole novel two years later.

Characters and Plot

The next parts of our re-introduction touch on a number of issues central to an appreciation of *Doctor Zhivago*. We start with the questions of characterization, plot, and genre, and then move on to the literary and cultural heritage of *Doctor Zhivago*. Such social themes at issue in the novel as the concepts of gender and ethnicity are then discussed. A somewhat complex question that receives consideration next is the question of time and history in *Doctor Zhivago*. A final problem treated here is that of translation and, particularly, what is *lost* when we read this work in English.

It has often been noted that, despite Pasternak's efforts at simplicity, *Doctor Zhivago* is difficult to read. The poet Andrei Voznesensky calls it an "anti-bestseller" (Bakhnov and Voronin, 231). The famous cultural critic Dmitry Likhachev hastens to explain this difficulty as one of false expectations: from the first pages the narrative style seems to promise its readers a traditional realist novel, easy to read, with a slow-moving, well-motivated plot and fully drawn, palpable characters. Likhachev suggests that *Doctor Zhivago* is not even a novel in this sense but rather a "kind of autobiography" of the poet's inner life, in which the hero is not an active agent but a window on the Russian Revolution (Bakhnov and Voronin, 175). Other critics have decided that Pasternak was even incompetent as a novel writer, as if, in the tradition of Henry James, there is a definite recipe that one must follow if one is to produce a "real novel" (Payne, 172).

It is tempting – and even reasonable – to start a discussion of character and plot in *Doctor Zhivago* by contrasting Pasternak's work with David Lean's movie, made in 1965. The movie, which is certainly more immediately accessible to an English-language audience, can serve as a photographic negative to help us define through contrast the particular nature of people and events, and the way they are presented in Pasternak's narrative. The movie offers clearly delineated characters and a conventionally well knit story line. In short, it is simple. There are many fewer characters in the movie than in the novel. The film focuses on five main characters: Yury, Lara, Pasha, Tonya, and Viktor Komarovsky. The medium of film stresses visibility: characters must be *visible*, which they are *not* in the novel. Interestingly, film critics who expected a monumental epic with a forceful, strong-willed hero were disappointed that these characters were so unheroic, so passive and unchanging (McInerny, 43). In this sense, the film is true to the verbal text: one of the mainsprings of the Pasternak work is the tension between the "epic" (the broad, "objective" view of a whole nation in flux) and the "lyrical" (the quiet personal vision). Nonetheless, in the movie we do see Yury visibly being a doctor and a poet: we see him making diagnoses, binding up wounds, publishing books of poetry, reading reviews of his work, and writing verse as well. In this way he is more palpable than his textual counterpart.

What is undeniably true about Pasternak's main characters is that while they are physically "effaced" (to use his own word; see his letter to Stephen Spender of August 22, 1959, in Part III), they seem to be more than just themselves; they have a strong symbolic "shadow." As the critic Anna Ljunggren has aptly pointed out, a character has fewer physical features, is more "effaced," in the degree to which he or she is spiritually close to the author (Ljunggren, 229). Major examples are Yury, about whom we know only that he is snub-nosed, and Lara, who is presented as light-haired and gray-eyed, but this generalization also holds for Uncle Nikolai and Tonya. These characters are "palpable" only through their physical movement, their own thoughts, and the impression they make on the people around them. We cannot *see* them as we can their counterparts in the film. Ljunggren notes a frequent confusion between these characters' speech and authorial speech. Conversely, the more distant the character is spiritually (for example, Komarovsky or even Antipov) the more visible he or she is. Pasternak's choice of the word *efface* (he wrote the letter in English) to describe his method of characterization is significant if we consider the central importance that the word "face" (*litso*) and the etymologically related concept of "selfhood" (*lichnost'*) have for Pasternak. Throughout *Doctor Zhivago* we find a sustained argument against types of any sort, social and ethnic stereotypes, archetypes, groups, and mass psychology. Each person has a particular inner "face" or *lichnost'*, a spiritually and morally integrated self that can be developed only in conscious interaction with nature and with another self – and to which all kinds of typologies are hostile. Thus, Pasternak has consciously muted the sensuous, palpable aspects of outer appearance and behavior in order to focus on the seeing, perceiving, knowing, thinking, receptive, answering and answerable "self."

Another idiosyncrasy of Pasternak's main characters is that they all seem to speak with the same voice. The Pasternak scholar Angela Livingstone claims even that the main characters "tend to merge, overlap and add up to a single mind" (Livingstone, *Boris Pasternak*, 6). This is particularly noticeable in the way that throughout the book Yury, Lara, and the minor characters Misha Gordon (4:12) and Sima Tuntseva (13:17) share the same philosophical discourse that Uncle Nikolai uses in part 1 (1:5). In this sense, Pasternak's book shows a family resemblance to the "lyric novel" of the early twentieth century, for example, Fyodor Sologub's *The Little Demon* (1907) or Andrei Bely's *Peterburg* (1916).[11] Unlike most "realist" novels, which are "dialogical" and show the emerging and often conflicting world views of several characters, the lyric novel is distinctive for its "monologism." Here a single authorial worldview predominates, and the narrative is generally structured as an allegory, a dramatization in social space and historical time of inner, private, spiritual experience. Despite whatever "realist" trappings it may have, this kind of narrative is about the world of the poet-author's psyche, and focuses primarily on the creative process within the psyche and the obstacles it must confront.

The plot of *Doctor Zhivago*, which so many critics have seen as its weakest aspect, likewise needs to be interpreted in terms other than that of the realist novel or the epic. Here again the movie can serve as a useful straw man. Let us start by charting the admittedly confusing mosaic of separate settings and historical events in the novel against the easier-to-follow, if historically and geographically confused, major scenes of the movie:

BOOK (dates approximate)	FILM
	1960s Soviet work site. Evgraf interviews young girl.

Part 1 (October 1901, the Feast of the Intercession of the Holy Virgin) – burial of Maria Nikolaevna Zhivago, Yury's mother. Summer 1903 – country estate of industrialist, Kologrivov.	Burial of Yury's mother in country.
Part 2 (October 1905) – Moscow railworkers' strike, suppressed by Cossacks. (December 1905) – Moscow, Presnya neighborhood barricaded, armed revolt.	Historical confusion (events of 1905 and 1912 treated at same time): Moscow. December uprising. Yury as medical student. Pasha at demonstration. Cossacks. Lara and Komarovsky at restaurant.
Part 3 (Christmas 1911 – winter 1912) – Moscow, Sventitskys' party.	Sventitskys': Lara shoots Komarovsky.
Part 4 (spring 1912) – Moscow, departure of Lara and Pasha for Yuryatin in the Ural Mountains. 1915 – Yuryatin, Pasha's departure for front. Yury at front in Galicia. February, 1917 – front.	Yuryatin: Pasha's and Lara's unhappy marriage. Two brief war scenes showing why soldiers deserted.
Part 5 (summer 1917) – "republic" of Zybushino; villages of Melyuzeyevo and Biryuchi. August 1917 – Yury's departure for Moscow.	Historical confusion: simultaneously Lenin in Moscow, provisional government announced, civil war announced.

Part 6 (late summer 1917) – Moscow. October 1917 – Bolshevik Revolution. Winter 1917–18 – Moscow.	Yury's homecoming.
Part 7 (March 1918) – trip to Urals.	trip to Urals.
Part 8 (spring, early summer, 1918) – arrival at Varykino.	
Part 9 (winter – spring, 1918–19) – Varykino.	Varykino: fall harvest, winter; Yury's trips to Yuryatin.
Part 10 (1919) – Western Siberia, villages along the East-West trade route.	Western Siberia: Yury's travels with partisans.
Part 11 (1919, fall 1920) – Western Siberia.	
Part 12 (fall 1920, winter 1920–21) – Western Siberia; Yury's trek to Yuryatin.	Return to Yuryatin.
Part 13 (spring–summer 1921) – Yuryatin.	
Part 14 (winter 1921) – Varykino. Lara's departure for Siberia.	Return to Varykino, Lara's departure.
Part 15 (1922–29) – Yury's trek back to Moscow. Moscow during the New Economic Policy. Yury's death.	Yury in Moscow, death.
Part 16 (1943) – camp, World War II.	

"Five or ten years later" –
Moscow. Misha and Nika read
Yury's notebooks.

Part 17 – cycle of poems   Postwar period at hydroelectric
                                          dam. Through interviews
                                          Evgraf finds Tanya, Lara's and
                                          Yury's daughter.

The movie's plot is simple and easy to follow for someone who knows no Russian history. Although it has been criticized for being a "soap opera" in which the revolution is used only as the backdrop for a love affair, the motion picture does reproduce Yury's struggle for personal independence "from the ideological maelstrom," simplistic and historically inaccurate as that ideological maelstrom may be in the film. And the film does try to dramatize the creative process and the impact of poetry on personal lives. It also gives some sense of lyrical structure through use of leitmotifs, particularly of the frosty window and the burning candle.

What the film would be hard-pressed to explore is Pasternak's play with the problem of causality that is the backbone of realist narrative and of historiography. Livingstone calls the narrative a "trance of interconnections": chance occurrences, coincidences, mistakes, and the like (see Livingstone, "Integral Errors" and *Boris Pasternak*, 61). In his essay here Boris Gasparov argues that linear causality is replaced by a more complex musical structure of counterpoint. Indeed, the novel offers no explanations and finds no causes for events either on the scale of national history (the revolution happens "as if by mistake") or in personal life, where characters meet by chance and where personal choice and strength of will play no role. Indeed, those characters like Pavel Antipov-Strelnikov, who do exercise their will, do so in a misguided way. Main characters have a strong sense of fate, of the conditions in which they lead their lives. Particularly Yury has to be moved to act; events happen *to* him. Only twice does he actually decide anything: once to leave the Forest Brotherhood and once to go back with Lara to Varykino.

And yet, despite this fatalism there is no overriding design of fate in *Doctor Zhivago*. Indeed, the notion of a network of predestination is travestied. The one image for the interlacing of individual lives is the chaotic and self-willed and whimsical telegraph operator, Kolya Frolenko in Biryuchi (5:10). Kolya controls all the communication in and out of Biryuchi: who talks with whom on the telephone, telegraph messages, train schedules and tickets. He talks in a transrational speech of Morse code, train talk and operator talk, that reflects all the different kinds of communication he must engage in simultaneously. In addition, Kolya likes everything to go according to *his* plan, and he is ready to stick out his tongue, both physically and metaphysically, at anyone who crosses him. This is certainly a comical, absurd vision of an absolute fate as the "little man," and yet it becomes dangerous and even tragic as Kolya arranges affairs in such a way as to encourage a fatal confrontation between the young officer Gints and the deserting soldiers who eventually shoot him to death (5:10).

The narrative of *Doctor Zhivago*, according to Krystyna Pomorska, is structured on the "principle of concurrence" – of lyrical association – rather than the epic "principle of sequence" (Pomorska, 81). In the process of making sense out of the "mess and chaos" of existence that is at the heart of *Doctor Zhivago* there is as much remembering – associating and alluding to earlier occurences, meetings, impressions – as there is a real forward-moving plot with some clear end goal that is somehow prefigured in the beginning of this work (Sinyavsky, 367). *Doctor Zhivago* is ultimately about the paradox that death can produce new life and that meaning can come from the debris of existence. Many Russian novels are structured like rivers: their plots flow in one direction – toward victory, say, as in *War and Peace*, or toward suicide, as in *Anna Karenina*. But *Doctor Zhivago* is more like an ocean. The very evident climaxes that do occur are not linear. Rather, they are really moments of revelation that happen when out of this "mess and chaos" one finds a pattern, a series of images, and an "immediate perception" that leads to the effect of transcendence, of self-overcoming (Danow, "Epiphany," 895). All these observations lead us to view the "story" of *Doctor Zhivago* as a cognitive process, open only to separate *lichnosti* in dialogue with one another, of arriving at insight about one's existence.

The Genre of *Doctor Zhivago*

The difficult plot construction, the characters' seeming paleness, and the "monologism" of *Doctor Zhivago* (that is, the characters' subjection to one single philosophical voice) all lead us to the major structural question: What is the genre of Pasternak's crowning work? One calls it a novel, and Pasternak thought of it as one, but is it a novel in any conventional sense? And what does the form suggest about how we are to interpret *Doctor Zhivago*? Using even the most capacious definition of a novel, that of Mikhail Bakhtin in such essays as "Epic and Novel" and "Discourse in the Novel," *Doctor Zhivago* presents problems. Bakhtin defines the novel rhetorically, in terms of the character of its discourse, as well as poetically, in terms of the nature of its structural images of place and time.[12] In both, Bakhtin sees qualities of being-in-the-present, flux, heterogeneity, and rhetorical tension (in contrast to temporal distance, isolation, fixity, monolithic and monological stylistic unity) as being central to the novel. Certainly, Pasternak's work is present-minded, and it challenges the ritualized epic past long consecrated in Soviet historiography. Still, its philosophical rhetoric is largely pronounced in one tone, that introduced by Vedenyapin in part 1 and carried on through Yury, Misha, Lara, and Sima Tuntseva. There never seems to be any challenge or risk *within* the text, except in Yury's talks with Antipov-Strelnikov and with Liberius, who ignores him anyway and thus will not be challenged. One risk is obviously in the collision between Vedenyapin's neo-Christian ideology of *lichnost'* (individual selfhood) and the Stalinist, "party-minded" herd mentality of the "official" reader; between the act of bearing witness to one's own historical truth and the reader who refuses to consider a rereading of history. *Doctor Zhivago* invokes two kinds of images of space and time: those of the biographical novel, with its inside spaces of family stability, and those of the road, the quest – except that here we find a kind of antibiography and anti-quest. Yury develops only in opposite proportion to family stability. Only as the family property is confiscated and he is separated from his wife and children does he develop his poetic and philosophical gifts. He lives increasingly on the edge of the abyss. And finally, as a self he disintegrates: as he abrogates family duty, deceives Lara and finally Marina. In that Yury is often on the road, traveling, the situation in *Doctor Zhivago* resembles the time and space coordinates associated with the quest. Except that the quest implies the will of the hero to *find* something. Yury is often under way, going somewhere, but usually *not* by his own will and not seeking anything in particular until toward the end, half by chance, he escapes from the Forest Brotherhood. A close reading of space and time imagery might show the productive tension in *Doctor Zhivago* of the antibiography and the anti-quest. In other words, in yet another way we may come to appreciate *Doctor Zhivago* as a challenge to the nineteenth-century novel.

Another approach to the question of genre is to consider that most unusual of characteristics of *Doctor Zhivago*: a cycle of poetry as the final chapter. Did Pasternak put in the poems to convince us that Yury is really a poet? Or did he invent a long narrative, as F. D. Reeve suggested, "to go along with the poems"?[13] Are the poems the residue of the narrative? Or, as Ljunggren suggests, is the narrative an enormous extension, structurally and thematically, of the poems (Ljunggren, 247)? The author of the screenplay for the film of *Doctor Zhivago*, Robert Bolt, thought Pasternak's work "less an ordinary novel than a disguised poem" (McInerny, 46). Henrik Birnbaum (1989, 290) has called *Doctor Zhivago* a *Gedichtroman*, or a "novel-poem." In his view, Pasternak's narrative prose springs from his poetry, operating on the same principle that Andrei Bely held, that "prose is the most difficult form of poetry" (Birnbaum, 291). It is interesting to note from the chronology of composition that the poems were written at much the same time as the prose pieces. In a way they are cut from the same cognitive and linguistic material. Certainly it is possible to show the connections between perceived image in the narrated text, Yury's meditation on it, and the transfiguration of it in poetic form. The most quickly recognized is the link between the narrator's description of the candle behind the frozen windowpane when Lara talks with Pasha before going to the Sventitskys' Christmas party to shoot Komarovsky (3:9), Yury's perception of the same image (3:10), the beginnings of a poetic line in his mind (3:10), and the poem "Winter Night" (17:15). Another is the link between Sima's discourse about Mary Magdalene (13:17) and the two Magdalene poems (17:23, 17:24). However, one should not press these connections between poetry and narrative too far. Instead, it may be more helpful to investigate techniques shared by both prose and poetry. For example, Elliott Mossman has usefully defined catachresis or "the metaphorical complex that results from wresting one metaphor from another" as a key to the narrative organization of *Doctor Zhivago* (Mossman, "Toward a Poetics," 396). Using the material of Yury's delirium during his bout with typhus and his later associations, he shows how an extended metaphor is "built out" relating typhus to nightingale song, Easter awakening, robbers, doom, and rebirth. In this way the complex poetic structure of associations underlying the prose narrative becomes much more apparent.

Lyric discourse may be dominant in *Doctor Zhivago*, but it is not the only discourse. It coexists with philosophical arguments about history, nationality, religion, and art, and with epic descriptions of social ruin. These parts are not represented in the final lyric cycle or chapter, which points to other nonepic and nonphilosophical kinds of order: the seasons, spring rebirth, the Gospels, and resurrection (Bodin, "Pasternak and Christian Art," 210–12). Still the three discourses bear a decided and deliberate relation one to the other. If the lyric has the "last word," and the philosophical may be said to support the autonomy of the poetic, then epic discourse, which occupied the highest rung in the socialist realist hierarchy of discourse, here occupies the lowest position. The argument could be made that in terms of its discursive and genre structure *Doctor Zhivago* is about the tension between the lyric and the epic in which the lyric impulse reasserts itself with a vengeance. Perhaps it is this tension between discourses and their strongly differing assumptions about human nature, society, time, and fate that really makes *Doctor Zhivago* a novel.

The Cultural Inheritance of *Doctor Zhivago*

Critics have often focused on the ways in which Pasternak's novel responds to the Russian literary tradition of the nineteenth century, particularly that established by Pushkin, Tolstoy, and Dostoevsky (see Erlich). What is increasingly becoming apparent is the degree to which the novel reanimates the rich and complex cultural atmosphere of the decades leading up to World War I. One might even argue that one of the unstated purposes of Pasternak's work was to preserve this world that the Stalinist apparat did everything to destroy. *Doctor Zhivago* represents the resurrection of that greatest of ages in the Russian arts, music, literature and philosophy; an age that after three decades, after the watershed of revolution, ended in diaspora and ruin. It was a synesthetic age, in which every kind of art form flowered – painting, architecture, theater design, music, opera, dance, and later, film – including, for the first time in Russian history, a flourishing religious-philosophical culture.

If one person could revive that spirit, it was certainly Pasternak, who grew up surrounded with art and music and himself had a gift for music, philosophy, and poetry. Pasternak's father was the well-known artist and illustrator Leonid Pasternak, and his mother was the extraordinary young concert pianist Rosa Kaufmann, who subsequently gave up her career for her family. As an adolescent, Pasternak was encouraged by the great composer Aleksandr Scriabin to devote his life to composing. As a university student, he spent several years studying philosophy with, among others, Gustav Shpet at Moscow University and in Marburg with Hermann Cohen – a pursuit he abandoned because he became disgusted with the compla-

cency of academic philosophers. But Pasternak's musical and philosophical inclinations are everywhere perceptible in *Doctor Zhivago*,
which overflows with remarkable voices and sound imagery, and
which is built on long disquisitions about history, art, and indeed the
cognitive process itself.

As the historical focal point of that era Pasternak recaptures that
peculiar mixture of mysticism and radical utopianism that characterized much of the "symbolist" poetry, as well as the religious and
political thinking of the first decades of the twentieth century. There
was a strong feeling of world-weariness, a contempt for conventional
"morality" and with the existing social order. The air was filled with
apocalyptic expectations. Leading intellectuals and artists were
nourished by the belief that social revolution would release powerful
spontaneous energy in nature and in human nature that would then
bring about a whole reordering of the world, the human psyche, and,
ultimately, life itself. The anarchist's bomb would answer the poet's
and mystic's yearning for new insight and new life.

Pasternak often invokes the name of Aleksandr Blok, the greatest
of the symbolist poets, whose long poems from the first year of the
revolution, "The Twelve" and "Scythians," resonate powerfully in
Doctor Zhivago. For Blok, as later for Pasternak, the historical events
of revolution are identified with meteorological events, particularly
snow and wind. But, most important, *Doctor Zhivago* gives a strong
negative answer to "The Twelve" where a gang of ruthless, leather-
jacketed revolutionaries become the Twelve Apostles led through the
wintry streets by the new Christ with a crown of roses (not thorns)
on his head; social revolution and spiritual renewal become one and
the same. In Pasternak's work, the revolutionaries, now partisans and
Red Army officers, are shown to be at best tragically deluded and at
worst violent monsters unleashed by the uprising.

Another theme central to Blok's poetry that would reemerge in
Doctor Zhivago is the problematic relationship between nature and
culture. The literary culture of the early twentieth century was built
on seemingly contradictory desires at once for renaissance and ruin.
Poets, composers, and artists claimed for their work a world-creative

power; they wished to break the bonds of the library, the concert hall, and the museum, to plumb the depths of the human psyche and the cosmos and reorder the life of the city. Nevertheless, their culture was fed by a death wish, the desire to find in nature a power much stronger than their art, which could blow the whole construct of culture and of the artistic ego to bits. Both Blok and Pasternak stress the thinness and fragility of the culture through which poets hoped to invoke that spontaneous surge of life-giving natural energy, which, in turn, could explode the very culture that had unlocked it.

Sexual liberation, as Jerome Spencer shows in his essay, was a burning issue in the first decades of the century. The strands linking social upheaval and spiritual renewal, natural catastrophe and cultural renaissance met at this crossroads. This issue emerges in part 2 as Lara is seduced by Komarovsky and as Yury and his friends Tonya Gromeko and Misha Gordon start a cult of chastity based on Lev Tolstoy's *Kreutzer Sonata* and Vladimir Solovyov's *The Meaning of Love*. Historically, the debate about sexuality was opened in the late 1880s through the scandal sparked by *Kreutzer Sonata*, a novella about a husband who kills his wife, in which current sexual mores are debated from a number of points of view.[14] Russia's greatest nineteenth-century philosopher, Vladimir Solovyov, joined the debate in the early 1890s with his essay *The Meaning of Love*, and offered Russian educated society a concept of meaningful sexuality that went beyond Tolstoy's stark asceticism. Solovyov founded physical love on androgyny, on the idea that both the man and the woman must acknowledge and accept in themselves the image of the gendered "other." One must accept the other not as an object of one's own desire but as a full subject in his or her own right – only then can sexual love have a regenerative aspect. One of Solovyov's central ideas was the feminine image of mystical, transcendent wisdom: the Divine Sophia. Sophia is a spirit, sometimes associated in the Holy Trinity with the Holy Spirit, that mediates between earth and heaven, and makes it possible for the seeking person to "know" the divine.[15] The closest one can come to knowing God is to know Sophia; and one can gain insight into Sophia only through "being in love," through surpassing one's narrow ego and gaining *lichnost'* or a selfhood in deep communication with the (gendered) other. All these issues and attitudes are played out at the center of *Doctor Zhivago* in Pasternak's staging of revolution, in the discussion of herd psychology and *lichnost'*, and certainly in the characterization of Lara.

One quieter, much less bombastic but nourishing thread of turn-of-the-century culture must be mentioned to give a more complete picture of Pasternak's reanimation. This is the quiet presence of Anton Chekhov, a doctor by profession who, until his untimely death in 1904, rejected the heat of the new mysticism and sought light in patient, clear-eyed, if often ironic observation of human life around him. As Pasternak wrote to the literary historian M. P. Gromov in 1948, Zhivago is also "a physician by profession but with a very strong second, artistic avocation as with the physician, A. P. Chekhov" (Borisov and Pasternak, "Materialy," 232). Chekhov, as the son of a former serf, was committed to the long-term task of overcoming the serf mentality characterized by the desire to "seek the master" and always to gain approval from some authority. This process was the core of his idea of freedom. Chekhov is an important model for Yury Zhivago in the sense that both are philosophically committed to clear-eyed observation of human behavior.

Gender and Ethnicity

Two social issues of enduring interest receive significant attention in *Doctor Zhivago*. These are the question of the status of women and of ethnic minorities and the legitimate claim of each to full *lichnost'* or selfhood. Both topics have elicited strong opinions from critics. We have said something already about the question of gender in Pasternak's work and particularly in *Doctor Zhivago*, but we can use this opportunity both to summarize and continue. It should be said at the outset that Pasternak was extremely sensitive to social abuse on the basis of gender and ethnicity in his own life. He was sympathetic to the plight of women who, he felt, were unfree in prerevolutionary society and who would benefit most from the revolution. Indeed, in

Spektorsky, the hero's sister is the active force in the family. She is drawn to revolution, and, indeed, the revolution is depicted as an "uprising of women" (Fleishman, *Boris Pasternak*, 156). Likewise, Pasternak, who was himself Jewish, was very conscious of the effects of Jewishness in his and his family's life. For example, in 1891, Jewish tradespeople were removed from Moscow. Pasternak's father did not have to go because he had a university degree and held the title of "honorary citizen" (E. Pasternak, *Boris Pasternak*, 20). In 1906 in his midteens Pasternak and his family left Moscow for a time because, as his father Leonid Pasternak put it, "the Cossacks were having a feast," reaction had set in, and Jews were easy targets (E. Pasternak, *Boris Pasternak*, 88). In contrast, in the 1920s he complained to Gorky that he felt that his tremendous success as a poet was due to the fact that much of the new literary establishment was Jewish (Fleishman, *Boris Pasternak*, 148–49).

There are a number of interesting points that *Doctor Zhivago* can bring to a discussion of gender identity. One is the androgynous character of Yury himself. Yury is not a traditionally "masculine" hero. Several of what Pasternak might see as "feminine" traits are predominant in Yury's character: his lack of will, his receptivity, his perceptiveness. His whole creative process is strongly feminine. In a Solovyovian sense Yury develops *lichnost'* through accepting into himself the female other: in part 1, it is his mother's voice (1:6) while later in part 11 it is his vision in the woods of the bannerlike icon with the female weeping head on it (11:7). Given that *Doctor Zhivago* is generally perceived as a full expression of women's experience and of feminine power, some contemporary readers have been disappointed to find that the experience and behavior of actual women characters are really quite limited and traditional. Yury loves to watch women do physical, domestic chores. With the exception of Sima Tuntseva, who is otherwise portrayed as a "strange" character, women characters are not thinkers or creators. Intellect is viewed by Lara herself as a domain in which men are superior. Yury does not give Sima the intellectual respect that he accords to himself and to Misha Gordon. When Sima does speak on philosophical topics, Yury does not do her the honor of listening but retires to the bedroom to listen through the wall. He soon notes to himself the dependency of Sima's thinking: "Of course, all this comes from Uncle Kolya [Vedenyapin]" (13:18). In general, women's creativity is limited to the biological sphere, to pregnancy and childbirth, while Yury gleans from these female experiences metaphors of creativity and creative inspiration. In the minds of male characters, particularly Yury, women are, as Barbara Heldt so wittily puts it, "reified" and then "deified."[16]

The situation with ethnicity and ethnic identity in *Doctor Zhivago* is also interesting and problematic. Pasternak is very sensitive to abuse of minorities, and *Doctor Zhivago* provides some moving descriptions of such situations, for example, the boy Yusupka Gimazetdin abused by the worker Petr Khudoleev (2:6), the scene of the Cossacks taunting an old Jew (4:11), and the mistreatment of Shmulevich the tailor (10:4). Still, in *Doctor Zhivago* as a whole, Pasternak makes an argument against all kinds of social grouping, national consciousness, and the like. In 1946, Pasternak wrote his cousin Olga Freidenberg: "In [the novel] I am settling accounts with Judaism [*evreistvo*], with all kinds of nationalism (including the kind apparent in internationalism), with all kinds of anti-Christianities and their assumptions – as if after the fall of the Roman empire there could really have existed genuine nations and they could really have formed a unique culture on the basis of some notion of essential national character."[17]

After condemning the Cossacks' behavior, Yury's (Jewish) friend, Misha Gordon, proceeds to argue that Jews, as a community, have become backward because in the "Christian era" there are no more nations: everyone is equal before God (11:12). Moreover, Misha claims that national groupings are merely a shelter for mediocrities. It is interesting to note that main and even secondary "minority" characters all become fully russified. Another ethnic figure, Galiullin, becomes an officer in the White Army. Misha ceases to worry about his ethnic background after World War I.

This debate – which, in contrast to his treatment of women characters and the whole notion of the feminine, Pasternak conceived *as* a debate – has called forth impassioned responses. In 1954 Varlam Shalamov thanked Pasternak for bringing up the issue (which had, indeed, never been aired in official Soviet literature, despite all the official attention to the "nationalities question"). He wrote to Pasternak: "The Jewish question in which everything is so complicated, is stated forcefully [in your book], and each person will have to confront this question consciously and clearly." Pasternak's treatment of this issue called forth childhood memories of a time when Shalamov's father, a Russian Orthodox priest, took the young boy to a synagogue and explained, "Look, there is the temple where people found God before we did. The truth is the desire for the truth." On the other end of the debate, George Gibian asks how it is that Pasternak can be so critical of Jewish ethnic identity and yet be so intensely pro-Russian in spirit himself (Gibian, 209). In a rejoinder the author's son, Evgeny Pasternak, emphasizes his father's religious and ethical approach to the problem; that is, his interest in *lichnost'* that ultimately effaces sociological identity. In general, on questions of gender and ethnicity, Pasternak holds to quite traditional opinions although he arrives at them in utterly unorthodox and original ways; in a cultural context defined by overpowering russocentrism and male domination, he shows unusual sensitivity.

The Meaning of History in *Doctor Zhivago*

Among the most tangled issues in interpreting *Doctor Zhivago* is the question of the nature of history. Almost everything about the view of history put forth here is ambiguous, both as it is implied in the "epic" form of the novel and in the philosophical conversations and life experiences of the characters. We have seen how Pasternak argues with the hyperbolic, heroic quality of the epic, particularly as it was used in the 1920s and 1930s, and how it forces diverse historical experience into one ideological mold. Pasternak implicitly disagrees with the standard "cake with cream" Soviet glorification of the civil war, and, well before anyone else in the Soviet Union or elsewhere, he offers a critique suggesting the behavior of the Red

Army and the secret police in the civil war was a precedent for the brutalities of the Great Terror of the 1930s. For this he earned the hatred of many radicals on both sides of the ocean.[18]

A large number of critics have dealt with the relation between Pasternak and Tolstoy, who wrote the most influential national epic of the modern era, *War and Peace* (Erlich, 1978; Gifford, *Pasternak*). Tolstoy is generally seen as being the great epic storyteller beside whose masterpiece Pasternak's work pales. We need to ask whether Pasternak is even *trying* to duplicate Tolstoy's achievements in characterization or in the description of battles. Or is he using his narrative, not to get the historical details "right," but to present quite a different concept of time and particularly historical time? Like Tolstoy, Pasternak disagrees with historiography that seeks to explain events by pointing to simplistic causes – such as the force of human will. But, in contrast, as Elliott Mossman shows, Pasternak takes exception to Tolstoy's mechanistic (and deterministic) metaphor of history as a locomotive, preferring the Darwinist, biological metaphor of natural selection (Mossman, "Metaphors"). Indeed, central though trains may be for the plot and the sense of poignancy in *Doctor Zhivago*, Pasternak carries out a thorough dismantling of the train as symbol of history. Although the train is pervasive here as an image of time and fate, it is remarkable how infrequently trains actually work! Typically, they break down, are overcrowded, are mishandled by the switchers and operators; and, of course, at the end Yury dies on a streetcar – a much-reduced image of the train – one that is airless, overcrowded, and broken.

Pasternak disagrees with Tolstoy on the issue of "progress" in history. While at the macrohistorical level of national and mass movements both would agree that there is no real progress, on the personal level Pasternak adheres to a three-part, "neo-Christian" view of history popular among intellectuals at the turn of the century (Clowes). This scheme argues for a distinct notion of progress: history can be broken down into three major areas, each of which builds on and integrates into itself the preceding ones. The first stage is the pre-Christian or Old Testament era of "law" when individual people have very little choice and are under the physical and mental control of the social group or of an authoritarian God. The second stage of history is the Christian period of "redemption" in which a person strives for social and moral unity with others through the Christian principle of "love of one's neighbor." The third period, of which intellectuals and writers at the turn of the century felt themselves to be the harbingers, is the modern period of free selfhood or *lichnost'*.[19] Now the self-conscious individual self takes full responsibility for all his or her actions but also is endowed with enormous creative freedom. Uncle Nikolai Vedenyapin presents this idea schematically in part 1, putting most emphasis on the first two periods. In Uncle Nikolai's concept, not only nations but individuals must progress through these stages in their movement toward fully realized selfhood. If historical events, as Pasternak represents them, appear to contradict this scheme, and instead return to some primitive, prehistorical state, then on the level of personal experience Uncle Nikolai's concept of history is more fully justified. We can trace the three stages in Yury's life as he dutifully attends to social and family affairs and later realizes his creative self in his poetic and philosophical writings.

A puzzle related to the concept of history in *Doctor Zhivago* is the question as to what Uncle Nikolai means when he says that in the second stage of history a person "does not die in a ditch but *at home in history*" (1:5, my emphasis). This optimistic view would seem to ring false in a novel dealing with a historical epoch in which so many people are made "homeless" both physically and morally. What does the opposition of history to nature mean in a novel in which everyone is reduced to a primitive, prehistorical level of bare subsistence, to the level of "nature," even as they participate in one of the defining historical moments of the twentieth century? Uncle Nikolai's phrase echoes a passage from Aleksandr Herzen's *From the Other Shore*, a series of essays on history and philosophy by one of Russia's most penetrating thinkers. All are in the form of a dialogue between a young person with passionate political views and an older, more

balanced and experienced intellectual. The younger of the interlocu-
tors, with whom Uncle Nikolai would agree, distinguishes between
nature and history. "There is nothing to be done about Vesuvius, but
in the world of history man is at home; he is not only a spectator but an
actor."[20] Uncle Nikolai implies that humanity is merely a passive,
helpless object in the realm of nature and necessity, but opti-
mistically suggests that people create history and thus can put the
imprint of an enlightened human consciousness on historical events.
Of course, for him, being "at home in history" is predicated on faith
in Christ and the Gospels, and on the concept of free and respon-
sible selfhood. The remainder of the novel belies this optimism,
showing how close natural and human events are to one another and
how little individuals can do on the macrohistorical level to affect
events once they have been set in motion. The main agents of history in this novel, Pasha Antipov-Strelnikov, General Kolchak, the
partisan leader, Liberius Mikulitsyn – all reject a morality of love of
one's neighbor and turn to a prehistorical bestiality (and, indeed,
insanity, as in the case of the partisan soldier, Pamfil Palykh, who
murders his wife and children to assure that a "worse" fate will not
befall them, that of captivity in the enemy camp).

Yury would probably agree with the second, older speaker from
Herzen's dialogue who questions the strict division between history
and nature and asserts that: "I believe that [man] is at home in both,
but in neither of them an absolute master."[21] This speaker seems to
challenge the opposition between nature and necessity, on one hand,
and history and freedom, on the other, calling these polarities "two
optical illusions." He insists instead that "the development of nature
passes imperceptibly into the development of mankind, that these
are two chapters of one novel, two phases of one process, very far
apart at the extremities, very close together at the center."[22] The raw
facts of history in *Doctor Zhivago* are about death and ruin and,
indeed, physical and metaphysical *homelessness*. Indeed, nature is, by
contrast, a force of life. The only freedom to be had is the freedom
to observe, to give things their proper names, to achieve insight into

what Sinyavsky calls the "mess and chaos" of existence, and to write these observations down for a later generation. Only by writing one's *own* history, by naming, remembering, and making sense, and by rebuilding the links between history and nature, can one hope to transcend death, as Uncle Nikolai had hoped. It is not Yury but his friends, Nika Dudorov and Misha Gordon, who have survived the Terror and World War II and are filled with the sense of imminent freedom (however fragile) when they read his books.

Doctor Zhivago in English Translation

A concern for any English-language reader will be the quality of the only English translation of *Doctor Zhivago* by Max Hayward and Manya Harari. Approaching it as an English text, it is certainly very smooth and readable. But we need to ask what is being omitted. Any translation pares down and distorts the field of associations that are invoked in the original. For example, in part 3, "The Sventitskys' Christmas Party," it would be hard to find words to impart in English the alliterative association in Anna Ivanovna's mind between an antique wardrobe (*garderob*, in Russian) and a coffin (*grob*). More important for a close reading of the text, the verbal repetitions that echo throughout the work and grow into metaphors and even long chains of association have often been allowed to slip away. In a strongly poetic work of fiction, where meaning is built through patterns of repetition and association between dissimilar things, this loss is ruinous. For example, a key word in part 1, and, indeed, throughout the novel, is the word *pamiat'* (memory) and its various derivatives. Memory is essential to the way in which each character introduced in part 1 conceives of himself and, in the case of Uncle Nikolai Vedeniapin's theory of history, how the self creates a sense of belonging in time. Memory is the central theme of this part, from the very first line, in which the mourners at Maria Zhivago's funeral sing "Eternal Memory," to the last paragraph of the final section, when Yura's young friend, Nika Dudorov, recalls a precious state of mind of earlier in the day. Unfortunately, this chain of associations is partly lost. The title of the hymn, "Eternal Memory," is translated as "Rest Eternal" (Livingstone, *Boris Pasternak*, 1989, 50). In section 6, Yura faints in the garden after hearing his mother's voice. Here a literal translation of the next phrase might be: "he was not without memory for long." Because this phrase was, perhaps understandably, translated: "he was not unconscious for long," it loses the connection to the problem of memory that is central to the novel and its concept of history and selfhood. This loss is particularly crucial since in this section the opposition is established between Yura's mother (whom he remembers and who is part of his growing sense of selfhood) and his father (whom he does not remember and even mentally casts aside).

In parts 2 and 3 similar strings of association are created that play a crucial role in understanding the experiences of major characters. The word "circle" (*krug*) resonates on a number of levels. The title of part 2, "A Girl from a Different Circle," is translated as "A Girl from a Different World." *Krug* here suggests different levels of society, the idea of social inequality. This idea is further borne out in Lara's seduction by Viktor Komarovsky, a rich, well-connected lawyer who travels easily from one circle to another. Lara perceives herself to be in an "enchanted circle" (*zakoldovannyi krug*, 2:14): she is caught and isolated by the charming Komarovsky. In the English translation this appears as: "What an inescapable spell it was!" At the end of part 2 when Yury first sees Lara, she and Komarovsky seem locked in a circle of light together, isolated from the rest of the world. Yury looks "into the circle illuminated by the lamp" (*v osveshchennyi lampoiu krug*, 2:21). Here the translators do use the phrase "circle of lamplight," but the associative field linking seduction to social inequality and injustice is gone.

A final example relates to the nature of Lara's physicality presented in part 2. One important associative link is the word for the side of one's torso: *bok*. With the death of their father Lara and her brother realize that "they would have to achieve everything in life with their sides," that is, with physical effort (*svoimi bokami*, 2:4). In the English translation this is simplified: "nothing in life would come to them without a struggle." This attitude is accompanied by the belief that any intellectual or spiritual labor is vain, only for the rich who have time to waste. As Lara starts to think through the effects of her affair with Komarovsky, she realizes that there is only abasement and abuse in their relationship, but no love. It is now that she starts to appreciate something other than the physical, the material. She goes to church and hears the Beatitudes for the first time and the support for the downtrodden that they offer. She develops a strong sympathy for the rebellious workers. It is now that she has a dream in which she is dead and buried in the ground. There are people singing a folk song over her. In this grave she perceives only "her left side and shoulder and her right heel" (*levyi bok s plechom i pravaia stupnia*, 2:16). Again this is translated without the crucial word: "there was nothing left of her except her left shoulder and her right foot." This is a physical position similar to being in bed, a position that she certainly assumes in her affair with Komarovsky, but now Lara associates it with death. This chain of repetitions of the word *bok* leads from unenlightened materialism to the beginning of her spiritual regeneration.

Lara's sensuous physicality is interestingly contrasted to the rather metaphorical, sublimated use of body image associated with Yury. Again the word *bok* plays a small but suggestive role. In part 3 we learn that Yury and Tonya have spent their childhood "side by side" (*bok o bok*, 3:10), and they know everything about each other. Here is an implication of equality: the two children are on one social plane. Moreover, implicit in this image is the notion that they have never touched each other. Thus, what Lara knows about the gender and power hierarchies in the world is a closed book to Tonya and Yury. All this disappears in the translation, which reads: "After six years of late childhood and early adolescence spent in the same house they knew everything there was to know about each other." To take this discussion of bodily images one step further, we can note that Yury's chief physical attribute is the eye, intelligent, observant, passive. Not only is he a voyeur of sorts (he is a poet), he also intends to write an essay on the physiology of the eye.

Conclusion

In 1959 the remarkable American critic Irving Howe predicted: "What Pasternak's views about the future of the Communist world may be, I do not know. But I believe that if and when freedom is reestablished in Russia, the people will regard him as one who, quite apart from political opinions, was faithful to the truth of their agony. And for that they will honor him."[23] Now, thirty-five years later, there is a good deal of freedom of speech and conscience in post-Soviet Russia. *Doctor Zhivago* has been published and republished in six huge editions. Including the original run of one million copies in *Novyi mir* (nos. 1–4) in 1988, nearly two-and-a-half million copies of *Doctor Zhivago* have been produced. Over the last seven years there has been a very lively discussion of the novel and related publication of correspondence and readers' responses. And now, it is well to remember, *Doctor Zhivago* is part of the new, post-Soviet literary canon.

Pasternak has a great deal to offer a new generation of Western readers. His style and worldview are as intriguing as they are difficult to pin down. While characters and events seem to function in a classically realist vein – they seem to claim full verisimilitude, to represent a "scientifically" founded, material reality – as the essays of both Boris Gasparov and Dina Magomedova show, they continually escape the bounds of this reality into the symbolic, the transcendent, the fantastic, the magical, stopping just short of the irreal. We think of the symbolic quality of main characters, the mythical nature of what we have called Yury's "anti-quest" for creative fulfillment – and still these aspects of the novel shimmer through a naive, matter-of-fact narrative tone. The strange and, to many readers, annoying accumulation of coincidences, the presence of fantastical characters (like Samdevyatov and Evgraf Zhivago, and possibly even the leechlike Viktor Komarovsky), and the transcendent sense of "fate" become more acceptable when we interpret *Doctor Zhivago* in the light of what in South American literature has become known as "magical realism." If the concept of magical realism emphasizes the void between the simple plausibility of the narrative tone and the irreal narrative events, then *Doctor Zhivago* is played out somewhere in the balance between classical realism, mystical symbolism (that seeks a transcendent consciousness), and magical realism. Pasternak's work never functions in the "irreal" world of, for example, Kafka's narratives, but it certainly shares a border with this realm. It never fully invokes the mystical, transcendent consciousness invoked, for example, in Blok's poetic cycle, *The Snow Mask* (1906), or Bely's novel *Petersburg*, but Yury certainly comes close to a vision of the transcendent Divine Sophia in part 1 when in a trance he hears his mother's voice and in part 12 when with the partisans in the forest he has a vision of an iconic weeping female head.

If *Doctor Zhivago* pushes beyond the realist expectations that so many readers have brought to it, it also goes beyond the modernist virtuosity its author practiced for so much of his career. In much of his best poetry and prose, Pasternak inhabited the very limits of language and of sense perception. He carried on a meta-aesthetic discourse about the nature of verbal art and its relationship to political and philosophical discourses. In *Doctor Zhivago* Pasternak brought these concerns – particularly the defense of poetry – to the people. Esoteric and inaccessible in some of his earlier work, he now tried to show the creative process and its poetic results in plain language. In this transporting of the rarified experience to the popular, "naive" level there is something of the spirit of the postmodern.[24] And something like a postmodernist spirit can be found in the ambiguity with which so many of the seemingly dogmatic philosophical pronouncements are played out, in the actual difficulty of Pasternak's proclaimed stylistic "simplicity," in the ambiguous balance among the desire for ultimate truth, the actuality of local, private truth, and the acknowledgment of physical and ethical relativism.

Whether or not *Doctor Zhivago* fits with our contemporary " –isms" is less important than that it deals with issues that will never go away as long as the tension between political or religious dogma and personal insight exists. *Doctor Zhivago* is the book of a survivor, a witness to the regeneration of the quiet creative spirit despite the most brazen and brutal efforts to repress it.

NOTES

1. Personal conversations with Vera Proskurina, May 5, 1994; Evgenii Pasternak, June 5, 1994.

2. Pasternak, *Sobranie sochinenii v 5-i tomakh* (Moscow: Sovetskii pisatel', 1991), 164.

3. *Ibid.*, 161.

4. Cited in *The Russian Novel from Pushkin to Pasternak*, ed. John Garrard (New Haven: Yale University Press, 1983), 221.

5. Boris Pasternak, *Sobranie sochinenii v 5-i tomakh*, vol. 1 (Moscow: Khudozhestvennaia literatura, 1989).

6. Pasternak, *Sobranie sochinenii v 5-i tomakh*, 4:208.

7. See, for example, Lönnqvist, 162–63, 172–78; Bodin, *Nine Poems*, 3.

8. Pasternak, *Sobranie sochinenii v 5-i tomakh*, 5:351.

9. Pasternak, *Sobranie sochinenii v 5-i tomakh*, 3:499.

10. This scheme is constructed from Borisov and Pasternak and the commentary to *Doctor Zhivago* in the new five-volume collected works, 3:641–81.

11. Johannes Holthusen, *Fedor Sologubs Roman-Trilogie (Tvorimaja legenda): Aus der Geschichte des russischen Symbolismus* (Gravenhage: Mouton, 1960), 18. Edith W. Clowes, "Literary Decadence: Sologub, Schopenhauer, and the Anxiety of Individuation," in *American Contributions to the Tenth International Congress of Slavists*, ed. Jane Gary Harris (Columbus: Slavica, 1988), 117–19. For a consideration of *Petersburg*, see Edith W. Clowes, *The Revolution of Moral Consciousness: Nietzsche in Russian Literature, 1890–1914* (De Kalb: Northern Illinois University Press, 1988), 164–66.

12. Bakhtin, *The Dialogical Imagination*, ed. Michael Holquist, trans. Caryl Emerson and Michael Holquist (Austin: University of Texas Press, 1988).

13. Reeve, 363.

14. P. U. Moller, *Postlude to the Kreutzer Sonata: Tolstoj and the Debate on Sexual Morality in Russian Literature in the 1890s*, trans. J. Kendal (Leiden: E. J. Brill, 1988).

15. Maria Carlson, "Gnostic Elements in the Cosmogony of Vladimir Solov'ev," unpublished paper.

16. Barbara Heldt, *Terrible Perfection: Women and Russian Literature* (Bloomington: Indiana University Press, 1987), 145–49.

17. Pasternak, *Sobranie sochinenii v 5-i tomakh*, 5:453–54.

18. Isaac Deutscher, "Pasternak and the Calendar of the Revolution"

(1959), in *Pasternak: Modern Judgments*, ed. Donald Davie and Angela Livingstone (Nashville, Tenn.-London: Aurora, 1970), 240–58.

19. See Nikolai Berdiaev, *The Meaning of the Creative Act* (Smysl tvorchestva, 1916; New York: Harper, 1955).

20. Alexander Herzen, *From the Other Shore* (Oxford: Oxford University Press, 1979), 75; my emphasis.

21. Ibid.

22. Ibid., 76.

23. Howe, "Freedom and the Ashcan of History" (1959), in *Pasternak: Modern Judgments*, ed. Donald Davie and Angela Livingstone, 268.

24. Guy de Mallac, "Pasternak's Critical-Esthetic Views," *Russian Literature Triquarterly* 6 (1973): 532.

II ❄ CRITICISM

Yury Zhivago's Readers: Literary Reception in Pasternak's Novel and in His Time

CAROL J. AVINS

The publication of many formerly taboo works was a major feature of Russian cultural life in the late 1980s, as books long kept from readers began to gain a wide audience. Discussion of this phenomenon of "delayed publication" encompassed fundamental issues, among them the legacy of censorship and the need to reconfigure postrevolutionary literary history. The task of revising the canon remains an endeavor as contentious as the canon wars in this country, if not more so. The phrase "politically correct" is relevant to both cases, though it means something rather different in the Russian context than in the American. With the former arbiters of ideological orthodoxy no longer in power in Russia, there has been a tendency to value most highly those works judged politically incorrect in the past.

Some critics have argued that recently recovered works are overvalued, the merit of their publication confused with their artistic merit. The 1988 publication of *Doctor Zhivago*, among the most prominent of these works, occasioned particularly lively debate.[1] But all the polemics surrounding the novel's reception omitted from view a noteworthy related matter: Pasternak's attention to the history and nature of literary reception within the novel itself.

Through his treatment of Yury Zhivago's readers Pasternak probes two central features of literary life in the Soviet period: how a work finds its way to the reader and how (meaning in what spirit, to what end) it is read. Each of these processes, dissemination and interpretation, can be measured on a spectrum of freedom and constraint, locating at the former pole the simple freedom of access to an audience and the more private freedom to make of a text what one will. The handling of these issues in *Doctor Zhivago* constitutes a skeletal history of the dissemination and interpretation of literature in Pasternak's time.

Before presenting the fictional forms of reception in the novel, let me take a glance back at the young Pasternak and a look around at the broader picture. Pasternak's interest in the relation between writers and readers – particularly between writers and readers separated by time – is reflected early in his career, in a brief essay of 1922 entitled "Some Propositions." His subject is the sources of art, among them the experience of reading one's literary forebears. He was translating Swinburne at the time recalled in this essay, and he marvels that the verse of Mary Stuart (read by Swinburne, who in turn is read by Pasternak) should retain enough immediacy and force to engender yet another act of creation: his own.

In a key passage he rejoices in the communality of sensation that a chain of readers keeps alive from one generation to the next: "This is what miracle consists in. In the unity and identity of the lives of these three and of a whole host of others (bystanders and eye-witnesses of three epochs, persons in a biography, readers) in the real-life October of who knows what year, that's booming and growing blind and hoarse, out there beyond the window, beneath the mountain, in . . . art."[2] In the Russian context the emphasis on October is significant: that month of the Bolshevik Revolution becomes a metaphor for any turning point, any time of transformation. Pasternak makes the point that no matter what October it is out there, all the Octobers that mark authors and their art are embodied in words and passed on.

There is nothing unusual in this idea. The history of literature is the history of reception, of writers formed by their predecessors, of nonwriters moved to leave the record of their reading not on paper but in other traces of their lives. Some writing fails to continue its passage through other minds, however. In any society many forces –

political, economic, aesthetic – shape what gets published, read, and remembered. To formulate the problem more generally: these factors condition what is admitted into the cultural memory, what is actively retained in it, and what is pushed to its fringes, thence to be forgotten or subsequently reclaimed.

Iurii Lotman has written that "[e]very culture determines its paradigm of what merits remembering and what is relegated to oblivion."[3] These paradigms governing the remembered and forgotten change over time. In some cultures, for some eras, another category of cultural artifact gains importance: that of works which are known of but cannot be printed or circulated. Such works engender what might be called a "reception legend," to propose a term analogous to the "biographical legend" posited by the Russian Formalist critic Boris Tomashevsky.[4] Just as the writer's biographical legend influences how a work is read, so the reception history of a work affects how readers respond to it. The special treatment given by Russian readers to once-banned books illustrates this reception legend effect.

Readers are not the only ones affected by a work's path to the public. Authors, in the course of writing, may be influenced by the *prospective* reception history of their works; they may know, for example, that a work in progress cannot be published in their own time. Pasternak and his contemporaries worked with an awareness of their contingent ability to reach the audience, and quite naturally for some writers this contextual factor became textual, taken up and explored within their works.[5]

How exactly is the contextual problem of reaching an audience at issue in the text of *Doctor Zhivago*? Who are Zhivago's readers, and how does the matter of his readership figure in the novel? That these are questions worth asking seems clear, to begin with, because the design of the novel in itself gives the transmission of Zhivago's writing substantial weight. The narrative's finale is a triumphant scene of reading with Zhivago's manuscripts at its center. Some of their contents – twenty-five poems – form the book's concluding chapter, thus satisfying the actual reader's desire for direct knowledge of Zhivago's literary voice.

To these obvious features of the novel's design I would add another. In the novel Pasternak ties reception history – the course of Zhivago's contact with the reading public – to national history as a whole. The reception of Zhivago's writing, each time it arises in the narrative, is linked to some crucial phase in the development of the Soviet state. There are four such "reception episodes": shortly before the February Revolution; in the early years of the New Economic Policy (NEP); later in the 1920s, as the Stalinist era was beginning; and in the postwar era, toward its end.

Each reception episode is emblematic of the nature of writer-audience contact in the period at issue. The episodes characterize only a certain kind of writer and certain features of literary culture, to be sure: emblematic is not encyclopedic. Pasternak deals expansively with some matters in the novel and approaches others by allusion and implication. Reception history falls in the latter category: these brief passages about reading form an elliptical plot that implies the rest of the story.

The "reception plot" opens with the young Zhivago's first appearance in print, at the very end of the prerevolutionary era. As he lies wounded in a military hospital in late February 1917, Zhivago learns that his two closest friends, without his knowledge, have arranged publication of a book of his verse. Pasternak conveys this information in a long and remarkable sentence that links Zhivago's literary path to the fate of the nation: "Yury Andreevich heard from Moscow that Gordon and Dudorov had published his book without his permission, and that it was praised and a great literary future predicted for him; that Moscow was going through a disturbed, exciting time and was on the eve of something important, that there was growing discontent among the masses, and that grave political events were imminent."[6]

One feature of this content-laden sentence is the relation between its two parts. A brilliant future is predicted for the young writer, we are told – and, in the next breath, an uncertain future for his country. What is implied by making Zhivago's literary debut simultaneous with the stirrings of revolution? To suggest two possibilities: Is the demise of the old order somehow a threat to the fruition of Zhivago's promise? Will revolutionary upheaval, on the contrary, enrich his art? The connection has more than a single significance: after all, the impact of the 1917 revolutions on Zhivago's life is in large measure the subject of the entire novel.

Zhivago's introduction to the reading public is notable not only for the emphasis on its political embeddedness, but also for the writer's lack of involvement in the event. This aloofness is indicative of his disinclination to become a professional writer, and it has at least one other implication as well. Taken in the context of Zhivago's subsequent publication history, the episode highlights the ease of access to the reading public in the prerevolutionary period. Even if an author failed to take the initiative, readers could arrange publication of a manuscript they valued.

To suggest that before 1917 all works had a clear path to the public is obviously a gross exaggeration: Russian literary history is full of writers' wrangles with publishers and censors. Nonetheless, the difference between this first reception episode and those that follow is telling. Although in later years Zhivago goes on writing and gains other readers, none reads his works in the form of a conventionally published book.

A look at his second encounter with the reading public, only five years later (15:5), reveals both Zhivago's changed relation to his writing and the impact of the revolution on the literary process. The early NEP period is the only time that Zhivago himself takes the initiative to transmit his writing to an audience. In 1917 he apparently felt no drive to get his work in print; now he devotes himself to writing and to arranging the publication of his work. The intervening years have been intellectually and artistically fruitful, and the more mature Zhivago has controversial, idiosyncratic views to express on a great range of matters: medicine, philosophy, evolution, history, Christianity. His essays, stories, and poems are printed in small editions as student projects by Zhivago's protégé, who by Pasternak's design is learning the printing trade. The boy thus serves as one of those fortuitous helpers (Evgraf and Samdeviatov are others) who facilitate Zhivago's literal and literary survival. Distribution, as well as printing, is private: the few copies of each pamphlet are sold in secondhand bookshops opened by the author's friends. We are told that they quickly find an admiring audience.

Why does Pasternak have Zhivago serve as his own publisher and distributor? In fact it was quite a common practice at the time (one contemporary observer describes how some Moscow writers even coped with the disruption of publishing by reverting to pre-Gutenberg modes, hand-copying and illustrating their own works.)[7] "Self-publication" – not the same thing as a later era's clandestine *samizdat* – was one sector of the book trade, along with a fledgling Gosizdat (state publishing house) and various private and cooperative ventures.

In this relatively unregulated climate Zhivago is able to disseminate his unorthodox works while maintaining his distance from literature as a profession. Though he is attached to a variety of literary and academic institutions, it is in the capacity of physician, not writer. He is not the talk of the critics, as before, but he gains a loyal following. This brief episode captures an important feature of literary life in the early twenties, before the lines demarcating the center and periphery of literary life were firmly fixed: one could publish by marginal means and yet not be a marginal figure.

By the end of the decade that was no longer the case, and Zhivago's wordless encounter with one of his readers – my third reception episode – tells part of the story. This scene, which hints at the advent of a new era of control over literature, is one of the novel's least discussed and most provocative.[8]

It takes place in an unspecified year in the late twenties, after Zhivago has become increasingly reclusive and has given up both literature and medicine. From time to time he does odd jobs, and it is on one of these ventures that he and Marina deliver wood to a man who is reading a stack of those pamphlets printed earlier in the decade. Though Zhivago does not know the reader personally (it would not be surprising if he did, given Pasternak's penchant for coincidence), he clearly recognizes the man's type. He is one of those intellectuals who have aligned themselves with the government, a path Zhivago himself has rejected. The force with which this scene is charged derives from the tension between the author's stance and his reader's. Here is the encounter in its entirety, beginning with Pasternak's description of the tenants of the apartment building where the scene is set:

> Some of them, particularly speculators who had made fortunes at the beginning of the NEP and artists and scholars who were close to the government, were setting up house on a comfortable scale. One day Yury Andreevich and Marina, stepping carefully on the carpets in their felt boots so as not to track in sawdust from the street, were carrying wood into the study of a tenant who remained insultingly engrossed in something he was reading and did not honor the woodcutters with so much as a glance. It was his wife who settled on the price, directed them, and paid them. "What is the swine so absorbed in?" the doctor wondered. "What's he marking so furiously with his pencil?" Coming round the desk with a bundle of logs, he glanced over the reader's shoulder. On the desk lay Yury Andreevich's pamphlets in Vasya's early Vkhutemas edition. (15:6)

End of scene; the narrative immediately jumps to another setting, with no further reference to this anonymous reader. The actual reader is abruptly left to confront several questions: why Zhivago reacts with such antipathy, even before he sees what the man is reading; why the reader is fiercely marking up Zhivago's words; and why, having seen his own booklets, the author fails to identify himself. All these questions are interrelated, and to explore them one must look further at the anonymous reader's identity.

He is presented to us as part of a new class: this building's prospering residents, whether traders in goods or ideas, are characterized as people adept at capitalizing on economic and political realities. This sets the anonymous reader in sharp opposition to Zhivago, who earlier in the same paragraph is described as having purposely fallen into poverty. Indeed, the opposition established in this paragraph is not just between writer and reader but between the two couples and their ways of life. In the roles of two woodcarriers in this scene, the unconventional Zhivago and Marina contrast sharply with the tenants of this comfortable apartment: the mistress attending to the household, the master to his work.[9]

And what exactly *is* this reader's work? Is his reading a part of it? And is he filling the margins with terms of assent or censure? The reader's absorption in Zhivago's writing might seem at first glance to be the stuff of pure intellectual passion. That interpretation is voided one line after its formulation, however, when Zhivago calls the man a swine – a startlingly harsh judgment, given the seeming equanimity with which Zhivago has accepted post–civil war Moscow up to this point.

Zhivago forms this instant judgment because he identifies the man as an "establishment reader" (to coin a label), a would-be arbiter of literary and ideological standards. That the reader sits furiously marking up a stack of Zhivago's long sold-out pamphlets suggests that this sort of critical reading is part of what his work entails. Perhaps he finds some of Zhivago's writing engrossing for its own sake. The dominant implication of the scene, however, is that the reader's purpose is to evaluate the status of that writing in these rapidly changing times.

That is why Zhivago's negative judgment is formed before he identifies what lies on the desk: he reacts not to what is being read but to the kind of reading in which the reader is engaged. Pasternak declines to address why, after discovering that his writing is at issue, Zhivago remains silent. One could cite here the view expressed by Pasternak himself around the time this scene may be set (1928) that the work of art speaks for itself, and that to discuss it with one's readers demeans them.[10] More to the point, however, is that Zhivago feels so at odds with this reader that he has no wish to communicate with him and his kind. That attitude explains his reclusive behavior in this period in general.

Given the paucity of detail in Pasternak's treatment of the years following 1922, only a few pages separate those freshly printed pamphlets with their enthusiastic readers from this strange scene. The strikingly different contexts in which Zhivago is read at the beginning and end of the decade illustrate the changing conditions of literature's existence. The emblem of the late twenties is the establishment reader, evaluative pencil in hand.

What of the reception of Zhivago's writing after his death in 1929? One presumes that the 1917 edition of his poems and those pamphlets of the early twenties are not readily available. But Zhivago's oeuvre includes unpublished works as well. His half-brother Evgraf, who avidly reads Zhivago before ever meeting him and who is Zhivago's most important reader, preserves his manuscripts until a time when they can circulate. As Zhivago's archivist he serves a function performed by other devoted readers in the Stalinist period – with the significant difference that the powerful Evgraf appears to be risking nothing. Evgraf is himself a member of the establishment, though he is no "establishment reader": in Pasternak's scheme he is an enabling reader, a reader provided by providence.[11] The involvement of this simultaneously familial and political figure in Zhivago's writing further illustrates how Pasternak ties Zhivago's literary career to the course of his country's history. This tie is made particularly clear by staging Evgraf's entrance (6:8) at the moment when Zhivago first learns of the Bolshevik Revolution.

We see the result of Evgraf's work in the novel's final scene. In the passage that concludes the epilogue, Zhivago's reception is again linked to a historical watershed: postwar regeneration. This is the last of the four reception episodes in the novel, and it features the same two readers who, more than thirty years before, had arranged Zhivago's entrance on the literary scene.

Now, in an unspecified year in the late 1940s or early 1950s, they sit once again with a single, unpublished copy of Zhivago's works before them. In this era, however, publication is not a possibility, not even the sort of small amateur edition that Zhivago himself produced in the early twenties. The notebook they hold, compiled by

Evgraf, is evidently the only form in which Zhivago's writing of 1922–29 exists. The medium itself tells part of the literary history of the years that followed.

To this inner circle of readers Zhivago's writing retains its contemporaneity and acquires a prophetic power. Contemplating Zhivago's words, Gordon and Dudorov experience the liberation to come; that is, the liberalization they imagine will develop in the postwar, post-Stalin period. To quote the epilogue's final lines: "To the two old friends . . . it seemed that this freedom of the soul was already there, as if that very evening the future had tangibly moved into the streets below them, that they themselves had entered it and were now part of it. . . . And the book they held seemed to know all this and to give their feelings support and confirmation" (531).

To say that the book "seemed to know all this" suggests that it has a supraliterary status, a potential to speak of more than its words literally convey. This potential is not a function of the long friendship between this particular audience and writer, but rather of the need of readers to find in the written word some authority for their own insights and inclinations. The way in which these posthumous readers sacralize Zhivago's work is illustrative of the way that taboo works are often read by those who preserve them. For Zhivago's readers a generation after his death, his writing is overlaid with material extraneous to the text – not only with the readers' knowledge of the writer himself, but also with their knowledge of the work's history, of all the hazards that these pages have survived.[12]

The prose narrative of *Doctor Zhivago* ends in an era when Zhivago's writing cannot circulate, but in the appended chapter of poetry the actual reader gains access to at least some of his archive. The inclusion of Zhivago's poems implies a reception episode beyond the prose plot: the actual reader's encounter with Zhivago's works (and with Pasternak's) after they make it into print.

This is the stage of delayed publication: the present stage of *Doctor Zhivago*'s existence in the former Soviet Union. As the reception of this and other previously unpublishable works has shown, even when the ban is lifted, the sacralizing, reception-legend effect lingers for some readers. *Doctor Zhivago*'s reception legend, given the sensational nature of the 1958 Nobel Prize affair, is likely to fade more slowly than most. But recovered works will not be forever regarded in terms of the path they have traveled to the reader. A new stage in their history will begin at the point when their reception legend loses force and ceases to affect the reader's experience of the work. The way will be clear for a more direct connection between writer and reader, a link of the miraculous sort described by Pasternak in that early essay.

However future readers read *Doctor Zhivago*, they will continue to find placed before them the question of what shapes a work's dissemination and reception – in twentieth-century Russia in particular. By embedding in the novel an elliptical sketch of reception history from 1917 to late Stalinism (a sketch that is partial in both senses of the word) Pasternak leads his readers to reflect on their own reading, and on the past and present realities of the literary process.

NOTES

1. In the flood of commentary that followed the publication of *Doctor Zhivago* in 1988, two articles stand out: Dmitrii Urnov's highly critical " 'Bezumnoe prevyshenie svoikh sil': O romane B. Pasternaka 'Doktor Zhivago,'" *Pravda*, April 27, 1988, p. 3, and the riposte by Andrei Vosnesenskii, "Svecha i metel'," *Pravda*, June 6, 1988, p. 4. Urnov's and six other views are translated in *Soviet Studies in Literature* 26, no. 3 (1990).

2. "Neskol'ko polozhenii," *Vozdushnie puti: proza raznykh let*, ed. E. V. Pasternak and E. B. Pasternak (Moscow: Sovetskii pisatel', 1982), 112; ellipsis in original. The essay was first published in *Russkii sovremennik* 1 (1922): 5–7. The translation is that of Angela Livingstone in her *Pasternak on Art and Creativity* (Cambridge: Cambridge University Press, 1985), 30.

3. Iurii M. Lotman, "Pamiat'" v kul'turologicheskom osveshchenii," *Wiener Slawistischer Almanach* 16 (1985): 7.

4. See his "Literatura i biografiia," *Kniga i revoliutsiia* 4 (1923): 6–9. A translation by Herbert Eagle, "Literature and Biography," is in *Readings in Russian Poetics*, ed. Ladislav Matejka and Krystyna Pomorska (Ann Arbor: Michigan Slavic Publications, 1978), 47–55.

5. Of the writers of Pasternak's generation, Mikhail Bulgakov dealt most expansively with this subject in his fiction and plays. For a look at how Bulgakov's approach contrasts with Pasternak's, see my "Reaching a Reader: The Master's Audience in *The Master and Margarita*," *Slavic Review* 45, no. 2 (1986): 272–85.

6. Boris Pasternak, *Doktor Zhivago* (Ann Arbor: University of Michigan Press, 1958), 130 [4:14]. Further references to the novel are given parenthetically in the text. Here and in other quotations I have modified the translation of Max Hayward and Manya Harari (New York: Pantheon, 1958).

7. Vasilii Nemirovich-Danchenko, "Kak zhivut i rabotaiut russkie pisateli," *Vestnik literatury* 3, no. 27 (1921): 10.

8. I am grateful to Marietta Chudakova and to Evgenii Pasternak for sharing their views on this episode.

9. This opposition is sharpened in the typescript draft of the novel (Pasternak Archive, Moscow, 338) which includes a fragment of a ditty composed by Zhivago that goes like this: "Raz u nuvorisha / V prazdnik Rozhdestva / S bednoiu Marishei / Ia pilil drova," and a loose translation that retains some of the rhyme: "Once at Christmastime / With my poor Marisha / I chopped a pile of wood / At some nouveau riche's." Given the somber tone and substance of Pasternak's final version of Zhivago's life in this period, it is surprising to find such humorous self-irony.

10. Pasternak makes this point in "O sebe i o chitatele," *Chitatel' i pisatel'* 4–5 (February 11, 1928). It is reprinted in *Grani* 53 (1963); a translation by Christopher Barnes is included in his *Boris Pasternak: Collected Short Prose* (New York: Praeger, 1977), 267–68.

11. On the sources of Zhivago's writing and on the revelatory function of Evgraf, see David M. Bethea, *The Shape of Apocalypse in Modern Russian Fiction* (Princeton: Princeton University Press, 1989), 265–67.

12. Lidiia Ginzburg makes some relevant generalizations about readers at varying distances from the time of writing in "Literaturnye sovremenniki i potomki" (1946), *Literatura v poiskakh real'nosti* (Leningrad: Sovetskii pisatel', 1987), 122. "[D]istant descendants affirm themselves by means of the work," she writes. "They can make no demands. They are pleased and grateful when they find material that serves an affirming function." The closing phrase of *Doctor Zhivago*'s epilogue – the remark that Zhivago's writing gave support and confirmation to the readers' feelings – uses the same word ("*podtverzhdat'*," "*podtverzhdenie*") that Ginzburg chooses to de-

scribe what distant descendants seek in literature. Gordon and Dudorov are, of course, Zhivago's contemporaries, but as readers they fit Ginzburg's description of distant descendants: they are removed from the period in which he wrote not only by literal decades but by enough upheaval to fill several generations. Their reading of the text is conditioned by the time in which they come to it. The survival of the work itself serves to affirm their own ability to endure.

Characterization in
Doctor Zhivago: Lara and Tonya

EDITH W. CLOWES

Critical discussions of Boris Pasternak's major prose work, *Doctor Zhivago*, usually identify characterization as a weak point of the novel.[1] If some characters are dismissed outright as pale and lifeless, others, such as the novel's heroine, Lara Guichard, are interpreted as symbols.[2] Pasternak was aware that his technique of characterization might seem inadequate. As he wrote in 1959, "more than to delineate [characters], I tried to efface them." His goal was to show individual fate as part of a larger reality, a "moving entireness" (August 22, 1959, Pasternak to Spender; see Part III). Juxtaposed to the palpable and plastic characters of Tolstoy and other nineteenth-century "realists," Pasternak's characters may seem less memorable.[3] My goal here is to go beyond the common evaluation of Pasternak's technique as a failed version of nineteenth-century realism, and to apprehend his particular concept of selfhood and his realization of it in *Doctor Zhivago*.

A useful way to arrive at an appreciation of Pasternak's experiment is to juxtapose his method of depiction of major characters with that of major nineteenth-century precursors. As Griffiths and Rabinowitz have shown, *Doctor Zhivago* emerges from the twin heritage of the national epic, both Russian and classical, and what they term the Christian epic of Dante.[4] Although Griffiths and Rabinowitz point out important aspects of the national epic tradition in Pasternak's novel – the broad historical narrative encompassing the coming-of-age of a nation, the integration of the hero's fate into his nation's future, the tension between "subjective" and "objective" private perception and public vision – they are less successful at defining the role of the religious, Christian epic in the novel. An analysis of Pasternak's techniques of characterization yields important insights into this question.

Before turning to Pasternak's characters, it will be useful to summarize what, in my view, is the essential relationship in the novel between the strands of the national and the Christian epic. While Pasternak in his novel certainly responded specifically to the Tolstoyan and, more broadly, the classical tradition of national epic, almost every aspect of the novel develops at variance with that tradition. The elements of religious epic emerge in confrontation with national epic; in the end personal, spiritual quest supplants monumental, national coming-of-age. The emphasis on the hero's external relationships to family, society, and nation of the national epic is eventually displaced by a more compelling inward drama of spiritual renewal and resurrection. This conscious departure from the national epic occurs on all levels of the novel. The novel's ideological orientation tends to interpret "history" not in terms of the heroic acts of whole nations but in the private, moral development of individual people. In the narrative, the depiction of sweeping historic events and broad movements of peoples, typical for example, of *War and Peace*, are reduced, giving way to Yury's and others' private visions. Yury's philosopher-uncle, Nikolai Vedenyapin, inspires several younger characters with his ideas about the "free personality" that dwells within history yet seeks to overcome history through personal resurrection. Finally, the novelty of Pasternak's technique of characterization is to show this private development in the few characters capable of surpassing the roles "assigned" to them by historical necessity. It is true, most characters in *Doctor Zhivago* are defined by their role in the historical events of the revolution. However, the two main characters, Yury and Lara, outgrow this role and develop a "higher" consciousness. They alone realize the spiritual freedom of which Vedenyapin speaks. To illustrate the development of Pasternak's idea of "free personality," I examine two symmetrically placed but opposed characters, Tonya Gromeko and Lara Guichard: one remains within a traditional epic role and the other grows beyond that role to achieve a deeper personal consciousness.

Tonya and Lara adhere to the female roles characteristically found in both classical epics and the Russian national epic novel. Epic heroines frequently appear in pairs of opposites. One heroine is what I will call a "conformist." She lives her life within the traditional social role of wife and mother. She enjoys what is traditionally viewed as a "legitimate," domestic relationship to the hero. The other heroine is a rebel or "nonconformist." She leads a life independent of the strictures of marriage, often developing a public personality of some sort. And she enters into what is judged to be an "illegitimate," extramarital liaison with the hero. Even in Homer's epics, *The Iliad* and *The Odyssey*, we find two women at least implicitly juxtaposed: Penelope and Helen. In Virgil's *Aeneid* we encounter Creüsa and Dido. Lev Tolstoy changes the double pattern to suit his moral views and artistic goals: Princess Maria Bolkonskaya is the major conformist, while Hélène Kuragina is the nonconformist. Although the heroine of *War and Peace*, Natasha Rostova, has elements of both types of character, she, like Princess Maria, is ultimately a conformist. Solokhov's *And Quiet Flows the Don*, a distant cousin of *Doctor Zhivago*, and part of the Tolstoyan tradition, also has two heroines, Natalya and Aksinya.

The conformist heroines, different as they may be, share fundamental characteristics. Each is a traditional wife. Creüsa is ready to follow Aeneas anywhere. At the end of *War and Peace*, Natasha Rostova is loyal to Pierre Bezukhov, and Princess Maria to Nikolai Rostov. Each gladly does her duties as wife and mother. Natalya Melekhova in *Quiet Don* is completely devoted to Grigory. She even attempts suicide when her husband abandons her for Aksinya; there is no life for her beyond marriage.

Each of these heroines is dedicated to the preservation of domestic and social tradition. In her own social context each is a conservative force. Thus, none of the conformist heroines takes part in the historical events that change the fate of both family and country. Because they are unable to adapt to historical change, many of them perish. Nonetheless, all sacrifice themselves willingly, urging their husbands onward to the new land. Creüsa dies before Aeneas ever leaves Troy, but appears to him as a vision, encouraging him on to unknown shores. Natalya Melekhova plays no part in the civil war, but waits patiently for Grigory's return. During the war she passes away, leaving him with two children to face the new world of Soviet Russia. It should be noted, of course, that Princess Maria and Natasha Rostova reverse this tradition. Both are survivors. Tonya Gromeko, like Creüsa and Natalya Melekhova, occupies herself exclusively with domestic life and family tradition. Like theirs, hers is an uncomplicated character. As she remarks in a letter to Yury, "I was born to make life simple and to look for sensible solutions" (13:418).[5]

The conformist heroine is always a loving and beloved mother. She bears children who cherish her memory even in unfamiliar surroundings. These women achieve a kind of immortality through the reverence of their offspring. For example, Creüsa, who dies very early, is remembered lovingly by her son, Iulus, as he, much later, fights for Roman lands. Similarly, Natalya Melekhova finds immortality in her surviving children.

It is significant that Tonya is one of the paler characters in Pasternak's novel. Her lack of distinction can be at least in part explained by her role as a conformist epic heroine. Typically this type is rendered inaccessible to the reader through a variety of narrative devices. She is almost always kept out of sight, her actions, such as they are, rarely occupy center stage, and her feelings are generally reported indirectly. For example, Creüsa speaks only as a ghost and exists in the memory of others. Princess Maria often appears as a kind of icon with "luminous" eyes. We learn of Natalya Melekhova's thoughts and feelings largely through an occasional letter to Grigory. In the early chapters of *Doctor Zhivago* Tonya is shown to the reader only as Yury perceives her. We appreciate his growing affection for her, especially during the famous dance scene at the Sventitskys' Christmas party. However, our sense of distance is deepened by Yury's lack of identification with Tonya. Yury always feels spiritually alone and apart from his wife. He feels he can understand almost anything, except what it means to be a woman. When she bears their first child, Seryozha, Yury compares her to "barque lying at rest in the middle of a harbor after putting in and being unloaded, a barque that plied between an unknown country and the continent of life across the waters of death with a cargo of immigrant new souls" (4:104). Tonya remains closed both to Yury and to the reader. Her apparent silence also deepens the distance between her and the reader. When she does express her feelings, like Natalya Melekhova, it is at a distance, through letters. She writes one to Yury at the hospital at Melyuzeyevo, in which she largely confirms what we already suspect: that she is completely devoted to one goal, tending to Yury's happiness. And again, in a parting letter to Yury, just as she is to be deported from Russia, her devotion and loyalty are given poignant expression. At the moment when Tonya will lose what she has always striven for – simplicity, peace, unity, a close family – she drives home the importance, indeed, the necessity of what has been forfeited. But, as before, Tonya is held at a distance from the reader: the letter, a completed (and, thus, in some sense, dead) document, and not the living woman, conveys the message. It is as if she, like Creüsa, were speaking to her husband from beyond the grave.

Like her epic counterparts, Tonya adheres inflexibly to tradition, unable to adapt to the new society. In the world of *Doctor Zhivago*, she is the only major character to remain within the old order. Her physical appearance, her family heritage, and her attitudes condemn her to isolation. Indeed, the trip to Varykino is only an attempt to cling to the past a little longer. Tonya does not even enjoy the immortality given others of her kind through the memory of surviving children; hers do not adapt to the new world. This privilege of the "conformist" epic heroine will be given to Lara, the rebel and nonconformist.

Tonya is a relatively flat character precisely because of her role as conformist epic heroine. She experiences few conflicts or crises that would provide opportunities for her character to unfold. In *Doctor Zhivago*, as in other national epics (with the exception of *War and Peace*), the personality of the rebel heroine develops more fully, in large part because of the dramatic possibilities inherent in her fate.

Socially and morally nonconforming women in epic literature all adhere to some degree to the same type. They are almost without exception intelligent, beautiful, and passionate people. Perhaps most important, all are "transgressors"; they strive beyond social and moral boundaries and are destined to meet a tragic end. These women are often prominent public personages. Helen, admired in all lands for her beauty, starts a war. Dido is the beloved and successful queen of Carthage. Hélène Kuragina in *War and Peace* is the center of St. Petersburg social life. As Tolstoy portrays her, Hélène is a travesty of the nonconformist type, using her social influence to undermine values of family duty and patriotic service.

Nonconformist heroines suffer a tragic fate. Victimized early in life by some more powerful figure, whether man or god, they themselves later violate moral and social convention. For example, Dido's fateful passion for Aeneas is forced upon her by Juno. In *And Quiet Flows the Don*, Aksinya was raped by a drunken father and beaten by a monstrous husband. These heroines find little joy in children, and their marriages usually collapse. Finally, their relationship with the hero, passionate and uplifting as it may be, is destroyed. Thus, in spite of their vitality and tragic nobility, they are condemned to perish.

It is interesting to note that authors of epics, with the important exception of Tolstoy, portray their rebel heroines with greater warmth than their conformist ones. Through physical description and dramatic confrontation they are made more palpable to the reader. Homer shows Helen great sympathy as does Virgil for Dido. The narrator of *And Quiet Flows the Don* is much closer and more sympathetic to Aksinya than to Natalya. On the other hand, Tolstoy, who puts married life and childrearing at the center of his literary world, reverses tradition. He invests his conformist heroines, Princess Maria and Natasha, with the vitality and warmth often given to a nonconformist heroine, leaving Hélène a one-dimensional character endowed only with calculating sinfulness. (It is curious and worth noting, however, that Tolstoy should feel sufficiently challenged by this type of character to choose a nonconformist transgressor as the heroine of an entirely different kind of novel, *Anna Karenina*. While repeating the same evaluative patterns – including two strong conformist women, Dolly and Kitty – Tolstoy nonetheless fails to reduce Anna to anything like the status of Hélène.)

In Lara, Pasternak counters Tolstoy's antipathy to the nonconformist heroine. Lara is warmly depicted, possibly with greater feeling than any other character in the book. The reader is allowed insight into her thoughts and feelings from the first pages. Indeed, she and Yury are the only two characters whose inner life unfolds. Pasternak makes Lara more than a traditional rebel-heroine by giving her the warmth, kindness, and sense of duty of the conformist. Although she is a vibrant personality, endowed with a strong will and love of freedom, she is very devoted to her husband, Pasha Antipov, and their daughter Katya.

In the general outline of her character and fate, however, Lara does adhere to the type of the nonconformist heroine. Like other nonconformist characters Lara is socially and politically active. While working for the Kologrivovs, she uses her hard-earned money to support revolutionaries, including Pasha's father. She becomes a history teacher in Yuryatin and later goes to war as a nurse. After the revolution she returns to Yuryatin and tries to reeducate herself politically. Although not a prominent social figure, Lara has a soothing influence on people and is adored by everyone.

Like other rebel-heroines, Lara leads a doomed existence. She is seduced early in life by the unscrupulous lawyer, Komarovsky. Although her passion, will to independence, and capacity for human love help her in her struggle with her unpromising fate, she never completely manages to free herself of Komarovsky's influence and the inheritance of her mother's subservience to men. As she remarks to Yury, "There's something broken in my whole life. I discovered life much too early, I was made to discover it, and I was made to see it from the very worse side – a cheap, distorted version of it – through the eyes of a self-assured, elderly parasite, who took advantage of everything and allowed himself whatever he fancied" (13:398). Even in marriage she cannot escape Komarovsky's shadow. She confesses everything to Pasha and devotes herself to her husband and child. Yet Pasha is unable to accept her love: he senses in her not true love, but a burden of guilt, a desire to redeem past sins. Even in the end, Lara is pursued by Komarovsky, who returns to Yuryatin to claim both her and her lover.

The epic fabula thus dooms the rebel. Lara is unable to find equilibrium in the new society. She loses Yury, only to recover his body after his death. In her wanderings through Russia she must abandon her daughters. Finally she is arrested and sent to the camps, where she perishes.

This picture of Lara's character and fate, while accurate, seems only partially correct. While Tonya does remain within the bounds of the national epic, Lara grows beyond her type to strive toward what Uncle Nikolai would call "free personality." She exists on too many other planes as well: the lyrical, the mythical, and the mystical. Lara herself at times appears as a symbol of suffering, sacrifice, and renewal.[6] In Yury's poetry she emerges "from her living prototype" as an iconic feminine image: "romantic morbidity yielded to a broad and serene visions that lifted the particular to the level of the universal" (14:453).

Physical description gives one clue as to how the characterization of Lara moves beyond national epic patterns. How Lara's physical presence is treated reveals Pasternak's understanding of free personality. Bodily attributes are used as more than emblematic shorthand, as is typical in the national epic. Rather, they link the character to a greater whole, a network of interpersonal consciousness. A good example is the treatment of Lara's shoulders and arms. It will be remembered that Hélène Kuragina in *War and Peace* is identified by her broad, white shoulders, which suggest at most the coldness of her personality. By contrast, Lara's are important; they play a role in her self-image, and they become symbolic of her connectedness with other people's consciousness and with the world of nature. Lara first becomes aware of her body shortly before sleeping with Komarovsky. She perceives her shoulder as she lies in bed: "Lara felt her size and her position in the bed with two points of her body – the salient of her left shoulder and the big toe of her right foot. Everything else was more or less herself, her soul or inner being, harmoniously fitted into her contours" (2:25). Her shoulder is part of a harmony of body and spirit. After becoming involved with Komarovsky, she dreams: "She was buried, and there was nothing left of her except her left shoulder and her right foot. A tuft of grass sprouted from her left breast and above the ground people were singing, 'Black eyes and white breast' and 'Masha must not go to the river'" (2:48). Lara's childhood peace of mind is crushed. Her shoulder here suggests inner emptiness.

Much later, in the depths of Siberia, Yury sees Lara's shoulders and arms in the snowladen rowanberry bush: "It was half in snow, half in frozen leaves and berries, and it held out two white branches toward him. He remembered Lara's strong white arms and seized the branches and pulled them to him. As if in answer, the tree shook snow all over him" (12:375). In all these passages the physical existence of Lara's shoulder and arms is their least important aspect. Their real existence is as a link between the consciousness of the isolated self and the greater wholeness of interpersonal consciousness.

Lara outgrows the national epic version of the rebel-heroine in still another way. Her nonconformist nature finds a certain legitimization through comparison to nonconformist archetypes of quite unepic cast. These archetypes are the women of the Gospels: the "fallen woman" Mary Magdalene, and the Virgin Mary. Indeed, through these two women, as Sima Tuntseva tells Lara, the Judeo-Christian tradition overcame the historic-epic mode of the Old Testament, which focused on the heroism of whole nations, and discovered a private vision that made possible the spiritual fulfillment of the individual. Mary Magdalene, an obvious transgressor, found forgiveness and spiritual resurrection in her love for Jesus. Sima points out, however, that the Virgin herself transgressed against social custom by having her child "out of wedlock," "by a miracle, by an inspiration" (13:413). Far from being ostracized, she became an idol and a source of hope. Central to the meaning of *Doctor Zhivago* is

Lara's reenactment of the drama of suffering and resurrection of the two Marys: thus, spiritually, if not physically, she overcomes her fate as epic heroine.

Lara's youthful affair with Komarovsky is implicitly compared to the experience of Mary Magdalene. Both women err, suffer, rebel, and finally overcome their sense of guilt. During a church service, Lara becomes conscious of her will to rebel against her heritage and her fate. She listens to the Beatitudes and realizes, "This was about her. He was saying: Happy are the downtrodden. They have something to tell about themselves. they have everything before them. . . . That was Christ's judgment" (2:49). Lara later becomes Mary Magdalene in Yury's poems.

Lara is more than a sufferer forgiven: she is a giver and a healer. In the last chapters of the novel, Lara resembles the Virgin Mary. Like the Mary of Russian Orthodox tradition, Lara is an intercessor (*zastupnitsa*). When Yury returns from Siberia to Yuryatin, he hears of "an exceptionally kind person," whom he immediately recognizes as Lara. This exceptional person, he is told, "always stood up for people" (13:387). The Russian verb used here is *zastupit'sia*, "to protect" or "intercede."

In Yury's imagination Lara sometimes appears as the Virgin Mary. While serving in the Forest Brotherhood, Yury has a vision of Lara as an icon of the all-merciful Mother of God:

How he loved her! How beautiful she was! In exactly the way he had always thought and dreamed and wanted! Yet what was it that made her so lovely? Was it something that could be named and analyzed? No, a thousand times no! . . . And what had happened to him now, where was he? In a Siberian forest with the partisans, who were encircled and whose fate he was to share. What an unbelievable, absurd predicament! Once again everything in his head and before his eyes became confused, blurred. At that moment, instead of snowing as had been expected, it began to drizzle. Like a huge banner stretching across a city street, there hung before him in the air, from one side of the forest glade to the other, a blurred, greatly magnified image of a single, astonishing, idolized head. The apparition wept, and the rain, now more intense, kissed and watered it. (12:367–68)

Here Lara resembles an image of the Virgin on an icon in a holy procession. This vision of Lara spurs Yury to rebel against his partisan warders and to return to Yuryatin.

In the final scene of Yury's funeral as Lara bends over to kiss her beloved, she is immortalized in a pietà-like image of Mary, the merciful, loving protector: "for a moment she stood still and silent, neither thinking nor crying, bowed over the coffin, the flowers, and the body, shielding them with her whole being, her head, her breast, her heart, and her arms, as big as her heart" (15:500).

The end of *Doctor Zhivago*, as Griffiths and Rabinowitz point out, stresses the failure of the national epic idyll. The national epic typically reasserts social peace through the reestablishment of calm domesticity. The woman again assumes the limited role as wife and mother. For example, Aeneas is to marry the young Roman princess. Princess Maria marries Nikolai Rostov. Pierre and Natasha are happily married and occupied with a new family. *Doctor Zhivago*, however, ends with division, disharmony, and discontent. Yury lives with Markel's daughter, Marina, and has two children, all without marrying her. Their existence hardly represents affirmation of social peace or prosperity. Yury is a broken man, preoccupied and absentminded, physically spent. He cannot make peace with his surroundings and eventually abandons his new family, to die alone. The disjunction of the new life is underscored by reminders that Tonya lives on in Paris, hoping for a reunion with Yury, while Lara sees Yury again only at his death.

By ending his novel with the cycle of poems of Yury Zhivago, Pasternak takes a final, essential step beyond the national epic and toward a personal, religious vision. The poems give still greater significance to Lara's rebellion and striving for renewal. In them unfolds a world of the spirit in which the nonconformist is no longer the doomed rebel as in the national epic, but becomes a principle of

life, passion, and resurrection. Several poems – "Belaia noch'"
(White Night), "Ob"iasnenie" (Explanation), "Osen'" (Autumn),
"Zimniaia noch'" (Winter Night), among others – celebrate femi-
nine vitality.

Two poems, in particular "Rozhdestvenskaia zvezda" (Star of the
Nativity) and "Magdalina" (Magdalene), focus on the experiences of
the Virgin Mary and Mary Magdalene. They represent Pasternak's
preference for the personal and seemingly unheroic over the national and heroic. "Rozhdestvenskaia zvezda" focuses on the miraculous, yet strangely simple and tangible, visitation of angels, Magi,
and shepherds to the young mother and child. Interestingly, Mary is
given greater attention than Jesus. The guiding star favors her and
her personal miracle:

> Вдруг кто-то в потемках, немного налево
> От яслей рукой отодвинул волхва,
> Итот оглянулся: с порога на деву
> Как гостья, смотрела звезда Рождества.

(Suddenly, someone in the shadows, touched the wiseman / To move
him aside from the manger, a little to the left. / The other turned:
like a guest about to enter, / The Star of the Nativity was gazing
upon the girl.)

The poem "Magdalina" is one of Pasternak's triumphs. Here
Lara's passion is expanded to a universal level. The hope, joy, and
suffering of Magdalene, as with the Virgin, is even more accessible to
us than the passion of Christ. The poem is replete with Mary's
powerful sensual desire, a desire sublimated as life-giving love.
Through her passion for Jesus she achieves a vision in which his
crucifixion, suffering, and resurrection become her own. It is Mary's
all-too-human hope for new life that we can identify with:

> Но пройдут такие трое суток
> И столкнут в такую пустоту,
> Что за этот страшный промежуток
> Я до Воскресенья дорасту.

(Yet these three days shall pass / And they shall thrust me into such a void / That during this terrible interval / I shall grow up to the Resurrection.) Through the experience of "falling," of spiritual doom, new life can be gained.

Through his technique of characterization, Pasternak does indeed "efface" his characters. Most remain well within the typical national epic canon, and thus may seem quite unoriginal. With a few others Pasternak deemphasizes or "effaces" specifically those aspects of personality – physical and social being – that were central to his great precursor Tolstoy in order to put into the foreground other, spiritual aspects of being. In particular, he renders physical detail an object of consciousness. With these few characters Pasternak animates his concept of free personality. He achieves his end by evoking national epic patterns of character development. In the case of his two central characters, Yury and Lara, he superimposes upon national epic types New Testament archetypes, with the effect that these characters are not only amplified but their fate is actually revalued. The rebel-heroine Lara is doomed in the context of an epic story in which national power and stability is valued over individual searching and growth. However, her striving is magnified and celebrated when seen in terms of the Gospel story. Through rebellion against the injustices of fate, through the struggle to know oneself, a person can hope to achieve that spirit of harmony, vitality, and unity with others that lies at the heart of Pasternak's idea of personality.

NOTES

1. Christopher Barnes, ed., introduction to *Boris Pasternak: Collected Short Prose* (New York: Praeger, 1977), 17; Vladimir Markov, "Notes on Pasternak's 'Doctor Zhivago,'" *Russian Review* 1 (1959):18; Mihajlo Mihajlov, "Pasternak's Doctor Zhivago," in his *Russian Themes* (New York: Farrar, Straus and Giroux, 1968), 253; R. E. Steussy, "The Myth Behind 'Dr. Zhivago,'" *Russian Review* 3 (1959): 192.

2. Guy de Mallac, *Boris Pasternak: His Life and Art* (Norman: University of Oklahoma Press, 1981), 197; Mary F. Rowland and Paul Rowland, *Paster-*

nak's Doctor Zhivago (Carbondale: Southern Illinois University Press, 1967), 44;

3. Henry Gifford, *Pasternak: A Critical Study* (Cambridge: Cambridge University Press, 1977), 181, 184.

4. F. T. Griffiths and S. J. Rabinowitz, "*Doctor Zhivago* and the Tradition of National Epic," *Comparative Literature* 1 (1980): 63–79; Robert Louis Jackson, "Dr. Zhivago and the Living Tradition," *Slavic and East European Journal* 4 (1960): 103–18.

5. Citations are taken from *Doctor Zhivago*, trans. Max Hayward and Manya Harari (New York: Ballantine Books, 1981). Part and page numbers are given in the text.

6. Jane Gary Harris, "Pasternak's Vision of Life: The History of a Feminine Image," *Russian Literature Triquarterly* 9 (1974): 410–17.

"Soaked in *The Meaning of Love* and *The Kreutzer Sonata*": The Nature of Love in *Doctor Zhivago*

JEROME SPENCER

"A love story for all time," declares the cover of a paperback edition of *Doctor Zhivago*. If that were all there was to it, we could read about Yury, Lara, Tonya, breathe a sigh, and then go about our business. After all, *Gone With the Wind* is also a classic love story, yet the many loves of Scarlett O'Hara may hold little scholarly interest. The loves of Yury Zhivago, on the other hand, have been the focus of countless studies and discussions. The reason? *Doctor Zhivago* is more than a simple love story: in the course of its many romances fundamental truths about the very nature of love are explored.

The discussion about love in *Doctor Zhivago* represents Boris Pasternak's response to a debate that raged in Russian intellectual circles more than fifty years before the novel appeared. Among the principal participants were Lev Tolstoy, whose *Kreutzer Sonata* condemned all forms of physical love, and the philosopher Vladimir Solovyov, who wrote *The Meaning of Love* in response to *The Kreutzer Sonata*. That *Doctor Zhivago* was meant to be placed within the context of this debate can be seen early on in the novel, when Nikolai Vedenyapin, thinking about young Yury Zhivago and his friends, observes, "The three of them had soaked themselves in *The Meaning of Love* and *The Kreutzer Sonata* and had a mania for preaching chastity" (2:39). It can be no accident that a reference to these important reflections about the nature of love occur a scant two sections before we learn of Komarovsky's seduction of Lara. Nor is it an accident that the novel opens in 1901, a year in which discussions about the nature of love played a major role in cultural circles. I will examine here the issue of love in *Doctor Zhivago*, exploring each relationship in the light of the argument about love between Tolstoy in *The Kreutzer Sonata* and Solovyov in *The Meaning of Love*.

But first, a brief discussion and comparison of the ideas of love presented by Tolstoy and Solovyov will be helpful if we are to understand the true "meaning of love" in *Doctor Zhivago*. We start with Tolstoy's *Kreutzer Sonata*. Written in 1889, *The Kreutzer Sonata* sparked a considerable debate about sexuality that penetrated Russian, European, and, indeed, American society throughout the 1890s. Among those who responded strongly was Solovyov, whose *Meaning of Love* was to exert a considerable influence upon such great Russian poets as Aleksandr Blok and Andrei Bely.[1]

The ideas expressed by Tolstoy in *The Kreutzer Sonata* are easily summarized. Through his main character Pozdnyshev, Tolstoy rejects all his contemporary society's ideas about love. The "love" on which marriage is based, he claims, is nothing more than a desire to copulate. Such carnal desire prevents any kind of spiritual relationship from developing (482–83), which is ruinous, as spiritual love represents the ultimate aim of human existence. Spiritual love, when it exists, is expressed "in words, in conversations, in colloquies" (489).[2] The only way to reach spiritual love is to eliminate carnal lust. With lust gone, spiritual love will dominate, and humanity's purpose will be fulfilled. With nothing left to strive for, the human race may allow itself to become extinct (491).

Solovyov addresses many of the same topics in *The Meaning of Love*. He begins by debunking some prevalent theories of love, revealing that only human beings can experience love because they, of all God's creatures, have the capacity for rational thought; only humans can be aware of "the Divine Image." The problem, in his view, is that too few people are able to recognize the "absolute significance" in their fellow human beings. Love, as the "justification and salvation of individuality through the sacrifice of egoism" (42), acknowledges the absolute significance of someone who is completely "other," that is, someone of the opposite gender (46).[3] The "other" does not, in reality, have absolute significance; instead the lover creates and sustains an illusion of such significance (52). In Solovyov's universe, it is always the responsibility of the "active" man to impart siginificance to his "passive," female, other (58).

Once the man has imparted absolute significance to his female other, true, spiritual love is achieved. This love is able to overcome death itself (65–66). Spiritual love is but one of three levels of love (levels defined also by Tolstoy in *The Kingdom of God is Within You*): animal, social, and spiritual, all three of which must be taken as one whole. They should be approached in descending order – spiritual affinity must be found first, followed by social and animal – and not ascending, as is all too often the case. Again, it is the man who leads the way through the levels of love (84–87). Women represent God's own "other," the "Divine Feminine"; when a man has reached a perfect relationship with a woman, he is allowed to become one with the Divine Feminine, taking Her characteristics into himself.

The Divine Feminine represents one crucial difference between Tolstoy and Solovyov; although both are looking for the unification of humanity in a "universal love," she is of critical importance for Solovyov, but completely absent from Tolstoy's thinking. While Tolstoy condemns physical love entirely, Solovyov assigns it a noticeable place within love's hierarchy, albeit only after a spiritual relationship has been created. Women are inferior for Tolstoy because men have turned them into sex objects; Solovyov agrees they are inferior, but they are so because of their innate passivity.

In *Doctor Zhivago* Pasternak responds to this polemic about love. Like Tolstoy, Pasternak rejects purely physical love, but, like Solovyov, he awards primacy to a spiritual love that might include a physical element. Rejecting Tolstoy's familial love, he also goes beyond *The Meaning of Love* to reveal what happens once the ideal relationship has been achieved; he disagrees with Solovyov about the nature of the transformation of humanity that love induces, and about the conditions necessary for such a transformation.

Turning first to the issues of love that Tolstoy addresses, Pasternak approaches the theme of purely physical love early in the novel. In place of Pozdnyshev and his wife, Pasternak presents us with the relationship of Lara and Komarovsky. There is only one major difference between the notion of physical love for Tolstoy and Pasternak: for Tolstoy, the effects of physical love are irreversible. For Pasternak, not only are the effects reversible, but Lara herself deepens spiritually, and Yury adores in her the image of the Divine Feminine. Even Komarovsky seems to salvage some humanity from his animal lust.

Komarovsky regards Lara in just the same way that Tolstoy claims all men regard women. She is an object of physical desire, important for her body and not for her soul. At their first meeting, he "stared at the girl so that he made her blush" (2:21). The first physical description we have of Lara emphasizes that she is "well developed" and "very good looking" (2:24). Komarovsky's astonishment at her "spiritual beauty" is revealed to be simple lust: "her hands were stunning like a sublime idea . . . her slip was stretched over her breast, as firmly and simply as linen on an embroidery frame" (2:45). His daydreams are of Lara sleeping on his hands as he watches her closely, an almost paternal image, but one that punctuates her submission to him. Waiters at his favorite restaurant undress her with their eyes. As long as she is involved with Komarovsky she is regarded as a sex object, not as a being capable of rational thought.

Pasternak emphasizes the parallel to animal existence emphasized in Tolstoy's and Solovyov's conceptions of physical love. Thinking of Lara makes Komarovsky pace up and down like a caged animal. Whenever he visits the shop of Lara's mother he is accompanied by his bulldog, Jack. Jack's appearances are few but memorable. In the first, he rears up and bites Lara, just as Lara herself is about to be bit by her animal, sensual nature. Jack is next seen walking with Komarovsky as his master swaps "dirty stories" with a friend. Their voices fill the air "with sounds no more significant than the howling of a dog" (2:44). Tales of sexual exploit are on the level of an animal, and a despairing one at that.

As Tolstoy would have predicted, the physical relationship destroys Lara. Before Komarovsky begins to seduce her she is "the purest being in the world" (2:24). Immediately after her "rendezvous" with Komarovsky, Lara feels, like Pozdnyshev before her, that something dreadful and unalterable has occurred: she sees herself as "a fallen woman" (2:45). And, again like Pozdnyshev, her remorse is tempered by excitement. She finds the whole affair flattering, fascinating, daring; it arouses "the little devil slumbering in her to imitate him" (2:47). At the same time, "a nagging depression and horror at herself" take hold, and she falls ill (2:47). She felt herself "sinking ever deeper into a nightmare of sensuality which filled her with horror" (3:71). Komarovsky is leading her to ruin, both spiritually and physically.

The primitive nature of physical love drives both Pozdnyshev and Lara to use violence as a means of escape, and here, it should be noted, Lara shows herself to be more active than either Tolstoy's or Solovyov's female archetypes. Pozdnyshev stabs the object of his physical lust, Lara attempts to shoot hers. Neither draws upon their rational nature to reason out a solution, thereby abrogating the very element that Solovyov claims sets humanity apart from animals. Lara's delirium is so intense that as she carries the gun to Komarovsky's she imagines the shot to be "aimed at Komarovsky, at herself, at her own face" and at her practice target (3:77). Distinctions have blurred and the only thing that matters is that a conclusion to the affair is reached. After her attempt fails, she spends several weeks in a fever.

The physical relationship between Lara and Komarovsky has done exactly what Tolstoy describes in *The Kreutzer Sonata*. It has turned pure Lara into a physically ill woman whose ability to make clear judgments is questionable. In contrast to Pozdnyshev, however, Lara's corruption is not permanent. She eventually transcends her depraved relationship with Komarovsky to become Yury's spiritual lover, going from the lowest extreme to the highest. Her evolution is not easy; as penance for her sin she devotes herself to others – to Pasha and her daughter, to the wounded at the front, to Yury – but she does overcome her fall. For Tolstoy, the only option for anyone, but particularly a woman, who has fallen is to "look on this first fall as their only fall, as the beginning of an indissoluble marriage," and realize that their ability to "serve God" is now severely limited.[4]

Pasternak clearly believes that it is possible to regain spiritual strength after a fall. Even Komarovsky, almost universally reviled by critics and readers alike, regains his humanity through Lara. Jack himself foresees that that might happen. He "hated the girl. . . . [He] was jealous of her as if fearing that she would infect [his] master with something human" (2:46). Komarovsky's brief pangs of conscience result in Jack's discomfiture. Komarovsky accuses Jack of wishing for the status quo of "mean tricks, dirty jokes" and responds by beating him up, attacking the animal – both his four-legged companion and his own inner nature – that prompts him to seduce Lara (2:46).

Lara's illness after her attempt at assassination finally awakens a feeling in Komarovsky that is not lust. He feels utter remorse at how "deeply, painfully, irreparably" he had ruined her, and resolves to "help her in every way" (4:91). Lara, too, notices the change in him (4:93). He is not "evil itself" as some contend.[5] He is as capable of redemption as Lara is; he simply does not remain redeemed.

Once she is able to put her affairs with Komarovsky behind her, Lara practically throws herself at Pasha Antipov. Lara never feels for Pasha the same love she would later have for Yury. Her love for her husband is more like that of a mother for a little boy than a love between two equals. Her first impression of him is that he is "childishly simple" (2:50). She describes to Yury, Pasha's "childish passion" for her and the desire she had had to "marry that wonderful boy" (13:403). Even after Pasha has become Strelnikov, she claims he is behaving "just like a child" (9:303). Her love for him, although strong, is too maternal to cause a Solovyovian transformation.

Lara and Pasha's marriage represents another commentary on Tolstoyan ideals. The ideal love of Tolstoy involves total devotion to the family (witness the happiness of Natasha at the end of *War and Peace*, and Kitty in *Anna Karenina*). For a while, Lara, too, is happy, for "this was exactly the kind of life she had dreamed of" (4:105). Her overmaternal approach toward her husband, "her kindness and fussing over him," quickly becomes a burden for him (4:106). Pasha is convinced that it is not him that she loves, but "the noble task she had set herself in relation to him" (4:107). He does not feel recognized. Tolstoy had time and time again argued that a woman's happiness could be found in the family, but what, Pasternak asks through Pasha, of the husband?

The same question is posed even more forcefully when we consider Yury and Tonya during their stay at Varykino. They live a near-perfect Tolstoyan existence, filled with physical labor that Yury terms "happiness" (9:277). Yet Yury is seeking something more; he keeps searching his memory for someone, someone who is always present in his subconscious. Significantly, he spends much of his time reading Pushkin, Tolstoy, Dickens, and writing a journal, but does not write any poetry himself. He desires to be "gestating something lasting, something fundamental" (9:285), but the constant cares and worries of family life keep him from doing so.

Donald Davie has attempted to equate Lara's relationship with Yury to that with Komarovsky. Although Yury's love is "pure" and Komarovsky's "unpure," both, he says, are sexual: "What is released in sexual encounter is *energy*, creativity as such . . . this is as true if the sexual partner is Komarovsky as if it is Zhivago."[6] This assertion is overstated. Neither Lara nor Komarovsky create anything from their relationship (in fact, their relationship drains energy rather than creates it; witness Lara's physical travails). Moreover, sex is almost completely absent from what we are told about Lara's and Yury's association. That is not to say that they were chaste; they obviously were not. But all the signs of carnality that were present during Komarovsky's seduction are absent when Lara is with Yury. Physical intimacy is referred to only twice, and even then indirectly: the first is where the narrator reveals that Yury is "betraying" Tonya, and the other when Yury suggests that they "speak to one another once again the secret words we speak at night" (14:428). We can only be sure with Yury's suspicion of Lara's pregnancy, and the probability that Tanya the laundry girl is their child. There is no reason to place the sexual intimacy of Lara and Yury in the forefront of their relationship, as it was between Lara and Komarovsky.

Just as the physical relationship between Lara and Komarovsky may be seen as an illustration of a Tolstoyan abhorrence of physical love, Lara and Yury's relationship can be viewed as building upon Solovyov's concept of spiritual love. Solovyov argued that the three levels of love – spiritual, social, and animal – must be approached from the highest level to the lowest. Without knowing it Lara and Yury follow Solovyov's idea almost exactly; rather than engage in "animal acts" first, they develop a spiritual connection that only later and incidentally becomes physical (and when it does, they also subvert the societal idea of family love by committing adultery). By subordinating physical love to higher, spiritual goals, they succeed in attaining the "perfect love" Solovyov envisions, although with quite different results.

Significantly, Yury's first sight of Lara reveals his disdain of carnal love. He sees her with Komarovsky and thinks, "here was the very thing which he, Tonya, and Misha had endlessly discussed as 'vulgar' . . . troubled and haunting, pitilessly destructive" (2:62). Contrast this with Komarovsky's first view of Lara and the difference between the two becomes clear: Komarovsky makes Lara blush with his lustful gaze while Yury finds the whole idea vulgar. Perhaps to warn the reader subtly of the parallel he is about to draw with *The Kreutzer Sonata*, Pasternak informs us that Yury is attending a performance of a violin sonata immediately before he sees Lara and Komarovsky.

Throughout their stay together in Melyuzeyevo neither sees the other as a physical object. Yury is afraid to appear "too familiar," while Lara notices his intelligence, but does not think he is handsome: he has an "unremarkable face" (5:125). In fact, Yury does not even know which room Lara sleeps in. Because they are not obsessed with animal attraction they are able to see each other as rational beings. Yury is amazed by Lara's ability to take "the highest human activity" – reading – and make it appear effortless (9:293), and to do the same with carrying water. Their time together is often spent in long conversations lasting entire sections. They are doing exactly what Tolstoy says should be done in a spiritual relationship: expressing the relationship in "words, in conversations, in colloquies" (*Kreutzer Sonata*, 489).

Their love follows the same course that Solovyov says would be taken in a truly spiritual love. Yury is the spiritually active one in the relationship. Lara, independent and active on her own, relies on Yury for decisions: go to Varykino or stay in Yuryatin? go with Komarovsky or stay in Varykino? As Ian Kelly points out, "when she becomes involved with Zhivago her role becomes more passive."[7] As Lara perceives their relationship, Yury, the man, has been given "wings to fly above the clouds" but Lara as a woman is given wings only to "stay close to the ground and shelter [her] young" (14:436). If Lara is to achieve unity with the Divine, she can do so only through Yury. He must, as Solovyov declares, "create and build his female complement" (84), and this is exactly what he does, by transforming Lara from a flesh-and-blood woman to a universal being, "an iconic feminine image" (see Clowes, "Characterization"), the Divine Feminine of Solovyov.

The transformation is slow and does not begin until he vows to end his adulterous affair, when he believes he will be unable to be with the physical Lara. He daydreams of her as the "dazzling, God-made gift of beauty from the hands of its Creator" (10:306). Just as Solovyov says God created His Divine Other for Himself (*Meaning of Love*, 91), so He created Lara for Yury.

During Yury's time with the partisans, Lara's image becomes in his memory "the gift of the living spirit" (12:345). Even more important, Lara becomes a part of him indistinguishable from his "inward face" – the unity of the sexes Solovyov dreamed about:

[He feels as if] the archetype that is formed in every child for life and seems for ever after to be his inward face, his personality, awoke in him in its full primordial strength, and compelled nature, the forest, the afterglow, and everything else visible to be transfigured into a similarly primordial and all-embracing likeness of a girl. Closing his eyes, "Lara," he whispered and thought, addressing the whole of his life, all God's earth, all the sunlit space spread out before him. (12:345)

Lara even appears to Yury in a vision – a weeping head, a "divine form" handed over by the Creator – reminiscent of Solovyov's visions of Sophia.[8] The appearance of his "inward face" as an "all-embracing likeness of a girl" is suggestive of another aspect of Solovyovian thought. In Solovyov's Unity, the seperate genders would be molded into one androgynous form. Both Yury's inner feminine image and his desire to create reveal that he, like Solovyov, wishes to become androgynous, to overcome the limits of his masculinity and to gain the abilities of his female counterpart.

Although the nature of Lara's and Yury's love is very similar to Solovyov's idea, the circumstances of their relationship are not the same, and here is where Pasternak begins to differ with Solovyov. Solovyov believes that "the inevitability of death . . . [is] completely incompatible with that elevated assertion of individuality . . . which is contained in the feeling of love" (Solovyov, 65). Love requires a physical manifestation; one can "love only what is living and concrete, and loving it in reality cannot possibly be reconciled with the conviction of its annihilation" (66).

Pasternak breaks with this contention on two levels. When Lara and Yury flee to Varykino they are aware that they are living on borrowed time, that at any moment they could be arrested and perhaps executed. Their relationship, however, continues to bloom even under the specter of seperation and death, which Solovyov felt to be impossible. Pasternak's second point of difference with Solovyov is a logical consequence of Solovyov's own theory. If a flesh-and-blood being is needed to discover the universal ideal, what happens when that ideal has been discovered? Yury goes on loving the ideal Lara, even after he has lost her physical self. Ian Kelly takes this analysis even further, suggesting, "In the end he lets her go with Komarovsky because she was becoming too 'flesh and blood'; her domestic roles were obstructing her Sophiological qualities" (Kelly, 215); he needed her to leave because "Sophia, or the divine principal, must always be 'in the distance'" (216).

Pasternak has one other major difference with Solovyov. Solovyov hoped for a transformation of humanity by spiritual love, but he held that a couple that had found love but remained isolated from the rest of society would not serve this end. The February Revolution finds Lara and Yury at the front, welcoming the beginning of a new society, chairing committees and participating in meetings. All of this, however, happens before they enter into a true relationship with each other. By the time their relationship blossoms into spiritual love, they are completely isolated. They are the "bourgeois" in a "worker's" world. Their journey to Varykino only completes that isolation. As a result, their love does not significantly change the nature of society, nor give humanity immortality in the manner Solovyov hoped it would. (Still, almost certainly Pasternak hoped that the image of Lara's and Yury's love would have such a "social" impact on its readers.)

The spiritual love of Yury and Lara results in a change of a different kind, one that fulfills the purpose of (if not of humanity's, at least of Yury's) existence. All his life Yury had longed to create a new kind of art, to write with a whole new style. When he and Lara retreat to Varykino, "his fingers itched for paper and pen" (14:432); he is possessed by the need to create. But again, it is only when the physical Lara has left that his creativity blossoms. He writes about Lara, but "the Lara of his poems and notebooks grew away from her living prototype" and became universal; the Divine Feminine is embodied in his work for others to read and experience. Once he has finished these works, the purpose of his existence is fulfilled. He must, and does, do as Tolstoy says humanity will do when *its* purpose is fulfilled: cease to exist. Thus his "going to seed," his spiritual decline, is the only path available to him.

Both Lara and Yury gain immortality through Yury's poems, the true "fruit of their love." Lara does so because it is her idealized image that is depicted in the poems, and Yury for the same reasons he outlines for his future mother-in-law, Anna Ivanovna Gromeko: "You in others – this is your soul," he tells her, "what does it matter to you if later on that is called your memory? This will be you – the you that enters the future and becomes a part of it" (3:68). Twenty years after his death, Yury is an important part of Gordon's and Dudorov's lives; the novel closes with them reading his poetry. He has truly gained immortality through his readers.

Throughout our consideration of Pasternak's views on love we have seen both fundamental agreements and disagreements with Tolstoy and Solovyov. Like both of his predecessors, Pasternak condemns a physical love that dominates a relationship, and, like Solovyov, he gives ascendancy to a spiritual love that incorporates elements of physical and familial love. On the other hand, Pasternak rejects both Tolstoy's ideal familial love and his belief that once sullied by lust a person can never be pure again. Pasternak also takes issue with Solovyov, arguing that the achievement of ideal love can happen in isolation from society, and with the specter of death hovering about. Where Tolstoy and Solovyov saw the accomplishment of ideal love as reaching the goal of humanity's complete harmony, Pasternak only sees the immortality of the lovers. In general, Pasternak's views of love have more in common with Solovyov's than with Tolstoy's; his acceptance of sex as a part of love is anathema to Tolstoyan ideals, and he seems to have accepted Solovyov's overall assessment of love. What is new from Pasternak is his redefinition of the end result of true love: the immortality of individuals, not of humanity.

NOTES

Citations from *Doctor Zhivago* are taken from Boris Pasternak, *Doctor Zhivago*, trans. M. Hayward and M. Harari (New York: Ballantine Books, 1981). Part and page numbers are given in the text.

1. Peter Ulf Moller's *Postlude to the Kreutzer Sonata: Tolstoj and the Debate on Sexual Morality in Russian Literature in the 1890s*, trans. J. Kendal (Leiden and New York: E. J. Brill, 1988) is entirely devoted to the controversy that surrounded Tolstoy's story.

2. Leo Tolstoy, "The Kreutzer Sonata," in *Tolstoy: Tales of Courage and Conflict*, ed. Charles Neider and trans. Nathan Haskell Dole (New York: Carroll and Graf, 1985), 473–530.

3. Vladimir Solov'ev, "Smysl liubvi," in *Sobranie sochinenii V. S. Solov'eva*, vol. 7–8; repr. Briussel': Fototipicheskoe izdanie, 1966. Citations are taken from *The Meaning of Love*, trans. Thomas R. Beyer, Jr. (Hudson, N.Y.: Lindisfarne, 1985).

4. Leo Tolstoy, "Afterword to the Kreutzer Sonata," in *The Lion and the Honeycomb: The Religious Writings of Tolstoy*, ed. A. N. Wilson and trans. Robert Chandler (San Francisco: Harper & Row, 1987), 74.

5. Mary F. Rowland and Paul Rowland, *Pasternak's Doctor Zhivago* (Carbondale: Southern Illinois University Press, 1967), 49.

6. Donald Davie, *The Poems of Dr. Zhivago* (New York: Barnes and Noble, 1965), 81.

7. Ian Crawford Kelly, "Eternal Memory: Historical Themes in Pasternak's *Doctor Zhivago*" (Ph.D. diss., Columbia University, 1986), 189–207.

8. Ibid. Kelly calls this idealization of Lara "pure Solov'ev" (207).

Temporal Counterpoint as a Principle of Formation in *Doctor Zhivago*

BORIS GASPAROV

For all the diversity of approaches to interpretation and evaluation surrounding Pasternak's novel, one opinion is shared by the majority of critics: *Doctor Zhivago* is a poorly made "epic": that is, it is not a novel in the full sense of the word. Some critics are inclined to regard Pasternak's novel as a failure overall, despite a number of isolated lyrical passages of unquestionable beauty.[1] Others, recognizing the great merits of *Doctor Zhivago* as an artistic whole, approach the novel as a work of lyric prose, not as a national epic. These critics regard *Doctor Zhivago* as an extended version of *Safe Conduct* and *The Childhood of Louvers*.[2]

If we move away from those features of the novel characteristic of "poet's prose," and turn our attention to the novel's epic components (plot construction, development of the characters, organization of the dialogue) it is hard not to conclude that the author indeed failed to build a full-fledged epic narrative. Here we find stilted dialogue full of cliché and sometimes in rather bad taste, awkward transitions from dialogue to monologue and from action to commentary, and, finally, an abundance of hackneyed, melodramatic situations. While it is true that deliberate use of the banal is by no means alien to Gogol or Bely, and melodrama can be found in any of Dostoevsky's novels, *Doctor Zhivago* surpasses these precursors both in quantity and in the degree to which it deviates from conventions of "good form" in epic prose. The most glaring example of this is the accumulation of all kinds of coincidences, chance meetings, and confluences of circumstances, which the characters themselves continually declare to be "inconceivable" and "unbelievable." Nonetheless, the coincidences actually form the mainspring of the plot: without the interference of all of the endless *dei ex machina* the action would simply not develop. Because this "poetics of coincidence" is much closer to the picaresque novel and to lyric prose, from that of E. T. A. Hoffman and Vladimir Odoevsky to the early prose works of Pasternak himself, we need to question the very inclination of critics to place *Doctor Zhivago* in the tradition of the realistic and postrealistic novel.[3] If we explain away these problems by viewing the characters and plot in terms of allegory, for example, as a literary transfiguration of the Apocalypse or Greek tragedy, we are left with a much poorer interpretation of the novel. Above all, an allegorical interpretation of *Doctor Zhivago*, in essence, represents one more way in which critics have rejected the novel as a work of full epic stature.[4]

All of these views clearly deny the significance that Pasternak himself assigned to his novel. A great deal of evidence from the poet himself, as well as his closest associates, shows indisputably that Pasternak considered *Doctor Zhivago* his crowning achievement, even to the point of rejecting all of his earlier work. What is more, Pasternak emphasized and reemphasized his intention of creating an *epic* canvas, the twentieth-century correlative to *War and Peace*.[5] Of course, an author's self-evaluation is often unreliable, and certainly so in the case of Pasternak, who had a penchant for underestimating and dismissing earlier works in favor of a work in process or just completed. Nonetheless, the questions of what Pasternak had in mind when he called his novel an epic and how this view relates to the real qualities of the novel both deserve further consideration. In this essay we look at these problems from the point of view of a modern reader for whom the realist novel of the nineteenth century, and even the postrealist novel of the first half of this century, are receding into the historical past.

————

There is no need to elaborate on the role played by music in Pasternak's creative consciousness. Apart from facts, illuminated in detail by the poet's biographers, both of his autobiographies clearly reflect his first creative experience in music.[6] But for all their expressiveness, references to music in Pasternak's poetry are comparatively limited, relating to a few and, in essence, stereotypical situations: the sounds of a grand piano, Brahms, Chopin.[7] A poet who was not so closely connected to the world of music as we know Pasternak was could have written about music as much and with the same degree of involvement.

The musical aspect of Pasternak's art is by no means confined to a few superficial, thematic references. After all, for him music was not merely an external phenomenon, serving as material for his literary art, but the medium for his first efforts at creative self-expression. We should thus be concerned less with what Pasternak directly writes about music than with how the deep principles of musical perception might have influenced the structure of his literary work. The quest for a musical theme in Pasternak must focus not on references to music but on the internal structure of his works. Seen from this point of view, *Doctor Zhivago* opens up exceptionally interesting avenues of interpretation.

At the very beginning of the novel Nikolai Nikolaevich Vedenyapin, the spiritual father of the protagonist, presents his conception of human history, which, in his interpretation, evolves primarily as a history of the soul: "Now what is history? It is the centuries of systematic explorations of the riddle of death, with a view to overcoming death. That's why people discover mathematical infinity and electromagnetic waves, that's why they write symphonies" (1:5).[8] Let us ask ourselves: in what way can writing "symphonies" be construed as a means to the ultimate end of overcoming death articulated by Vedenyapin? One of the salient features of music in general, and particularly for music in this century, with its heightened interest in the regeneration and development of all kinds of polyphonic forms, is its ability to deal simultaneously with several melodic lines whose development differs in time. Interrelations between different voices, that had started at different points of the composition and progressed with different speed, create infinite possibilities for variation, with different melodic lines sometimes diverging far from one another, and sometimes merging into one. Psychologically and symbolically this whole process can be interpreted as an *overcoming of the linear flow of time*: owing to the simultaneous perception of lines flowing at different rates, that is, as though in different temporal phases of development, the listener proves capable of escaping a unidirectional, uniform, and irreversible temporal flow, and by doing so can also symbolically overcome time, and, by association, "overcome death."

The effect of nonlinearity, or "polyphony," is to some degree characteristic of all types of art, and it has repeatedly been singled out as a principle central to Pasternak's prose works.[9] It is worth emphasizing, however, that polyphony is fully realized primarily in music, and in music it becomes a universal organizing principle that holds the whole composition together. Thus, in his monologue Vedenyapin refers specifically to "symphonies," although, of course, all other forms of art contribute to the spiritual solution of the problem that he posed. It is no accident that the greatest novelists of this century, in devoting themselves to an intense "search for a bygone time," felt the strong influence of music on their artistic world – an influence realized less in direct references to musical impressions than in the use of such musical forms as the symphony, the fugue, and the oratorio, and the principles of musical composition for the creation of new foundations for epic form. Aldous Huxley called this phenomenon "the musicalization of fiction: not in the symbolist way, by subordinating sense to sound, . . . but on a large scale, in the construction."[10] Besides Huxley, we must mention in this connection Andrei Bely, Proust, Bulgakov, Thomas Mann.[11] And to their number must be added Pasternak.

––––

The whole of *Doctor Zhivago* is structured on the "contrapuntal" principle of irregular movement of time and "relativity" of various events progressing at different speeds. This temporal counterpoint assumes two forms in Pasternak. The first and simpler of the two is characterized by the unevenness of a single temporal movement linking together a series of events of deliberately uneven, changeable rhythm. The movement of a train is used as a favorite image to express this idea. In the novel trains always move unevenly, a detail, of course, quite plausible for the historical period represented. Trains first gather great speed, then come to a stop for an unpredictably long period of time. This unevenness of movement corresponds to sudden changes of lighting, perspective, sound, and also the consciousness of the hero, Yury Zhivago.

The other form of temporal counterpoint in *Doctor Zhivago*, even more broadly developed, consists of the combination of several lines of events, each moving at a different speed with its own rhythm and direction. If one train alone is emblematic of the first type of counterpoint, then the "railroad timetable" is an appropriate emblem for the second: the polyphony of the central railroad station and the provincial railway depot. Apart from the role that way stations, large city stations, and small depots play in the plot of the novel (as well as in Pasternak's poetry), is the extremely important role in the poet's life of Astapovo Station (where Lev Tolstoy died in 1910), the place where the young Pasternak crossed paths with the poet Rainer Maria Rilke and Tolstoy.[12]

The image of movement in its literal everyday meaning – the movement of a train, a streetcar, pedestrians, the journey of Zhivago in a sleeping car through Siberia, and so forth – serves only as a starting point for contrapuntal constructions. These images can absorb into themselves the most diverse metaphorical transformations of the general contrapuntal idea: the movement of days and seasons, the shifts in historical epochs and chronology itself, trends in natural science and metaphysics, the progress of individual human fates (the "paths of their lives"), and, finally, the rhythmical pace of various poetic meters and different forms of narrative.

One of the final scenes of the novel can serve as an example of the merging of these diverse figurative lines into a single counterpoint: Zhivago is traveling on a tram that moves haltingly, stopping every now and then. Along the sidewalk parallel to the tram walks an old woman, Mademoiselle Fleury, who sometimes lags behind the tram and sometimes overtakes and passes it. This conflict between various kinds of locomotion is also reflected in nature in the struggle between the intense heat and an approaching cloud (the "purple" color of which corresponds to the "violet" dress of the woman) and in the psychological and physical state of the protagonist; his heart works unevenly and haltingly, and his thoughts are "confused." The intermittent beating of his heart calls forth in Zhivago the thought of death. This thought joins with the figure of the "gray old lady" and the classical mathematical problem about the movement of two travelers to bring Zhivago to his formulation of the "principle of relativity at life's hippodrome." This idiom in turn allows us to correlate the ideas of fate and a horse race still more precisely: "He tried to imagine several people whose lives run parallel and close together but move at different speeds, and he wondered in what circumstances some of them would overtake and survive others" (15:12).

In the end the parallel flow of so many semantic lines leads to a another "surprising" coincidence so typical for the poetics of this novel, but really no more surprising than the coincidence of various lines in a polyphonic composition merging into a chord. Zhivago jumps out of the streetcar, which has stopped once again, and drops dead. Just as at the beginning of the novel the stop of the express train indicated the death of his father. the streetcar's stopping coincides here with the failure of his heart and the end of his "life's journey." Also, the "very old" Mademoiselle Fleury again overtakes the streetcar, remaining "quite unaware that she had overtaken Zhivago and survived him." Finally, the storm begins: the "purple cloud" triumphs in nature. It is important to note that storms are widespread in mythology as the archetypal symbol of the duel of the sacral hero, for example, Persius, Perun, or Saint George, with the snake, cloud, or dragon. It corresponds to a central image that appears in the Zhivago poems and also to a whole sequence of incidents that describe the relations of Yury and Lara.[13]

Another good example of counterpoint can be found in the novel's principal symbol of movement: the train. The train, bound from

Moscow for Yuryatin, stops at night at an unknown point where Zhivago's attention is drawn to the unexpected silence reigning over everything. It is as if this silence had carried him to a different epoch, the years before the war when people on the platform were considerate of the people sleeping in the train: "The doctor was mistaken. There was the same din of shouting voices and stamping boots on this platform as on any other. But there was a waterfall near by. It widened the expanse of the white night by a breath of freshness and freedom; that was what had filled him with happiness in his sleep. Its incessant noise dominated all other sounds and gave an illusion of stillness" (7:21).

In this episode the "relativity" of sound impressions (that is, the strongest sound overcomes all the other sounds and turns them into silence) and the key image of irregular motion along the rails invoke a whole set of contrapuntal superimpositions: the juxtaposition of two epochs, various spatial rhythms, such as the effect of "expanding" space, the transition from dreaming to waking, and the sudden shift of the mood of the protagonist that conveys the first premonition of the coming spring, a theme that is to be developed further in the same part.

Just as the noise of the waterfall turns all other sounds into silence, the enormous speed of revolutionary events creates the illusion that the flow of daily life has completely stopped, that "nothing is happening in the world." Only afterward, when this intensive historical rhythm dies down, do the characters find out "that for these five or ten years they survived more than others do in an entire century" (6:4). Once again, as with Zhivago's final thoughts in the streetcar, the theory of relativity is brought to bear, and in particular, its popular literary representation in the image of the inhabitants of a spaceship whose objective time appears to have many times the capacity of time on earth. The "principle of relativity" applies here not to individual fates, as in the streetcar scene, but to the movement of historical epochs. The disparity in the flow of time in various epochs is underscored by such inconspicuous, but characteristic details as the mention of the two calendars, Gregorian and Julian – for example, the narrator refers to "the sixth of August according to the old calendar" – and of the double manner of telling time, for example, "at the seventh hour according to liturgical time, but according to common calculation, at one in the night."[14]

In the same way as they embrace individual fates, historical events, the life of nature, and the cosmic order, contrapuntal constructions also include aesthetic phenomena: the flow of various poetic measures and distinct types of narrative. As Yury notes in his journal (part 9), the short and long lines in Pushkin's early poetry correspond to more or less condensed meaning and the progress of the adolescent author toward artistic maturity. The flow of trisyllabic "Nekrasovian" meters, in contrast to Pushkin's iambs, serves as a rhythmical "measure" of a later historical epoch. Historical epochs move in different rhythms, and the flow of meters changes correspondingly: the declamatory iamb confronts the dactylic representation of "melodic speech." Finally, these different modes of speech can be polyphonically combined with each other. We find this kind of combination, for example, in Zhivago's double monologue after his parting with Lara: "He went into the house. A double monologue was going on in his mind, two different kinds of monologue, the one dry and businesslike, the other addressed to Lara, like a river in flood" (14:13).

The broadest use of counterpoint can be seen in the construction of the novel as a whole. The texture of *Doctor Zhivago* is created through the combination and superimposition of various types of artistic speech that evolve in different temporal and semantic rhythms. Most important are lyric and prose. Within the limits of these two discourses are found various genres and styles, both innovative and traditional, high and low: philosophical lyric poetry and ballad, objective narrative and subjective romantic prose, the historical epic and the melodramatic tale reminiscent of Dostoevsky's "The Landlady," the fairy tale and the naturalist sketch of urban life.[15] At first glance this colorful mix can easily be taken for unevenness of style and falseness of form.

The diametric opposite of counterpoint is the unity and fusion of all voices, a kind of "singing in unison." Phenomena of this sort are invariably treated very negatively in *Doctor Zhivago*. At one point Lara literally speaks of the idea of mass psychological conformity in terms of a choir singing in unison: "People imagined . . . that now it was necessary to sing with a single voice and to live as strangers who are all tied together by ideas" (13:14). At another point she describes a similar phenomenon in direct opposition to the "interweaving" of voices characteristic of real life and genuine art: "It's only in mediocre books that people are divided into two camps and have nothing to do with each other. In real life everything gets mixed up! Don't you think you'd have to be a hopeless nonentity to play only one role all your life, to have only one place in society, always to stand for the same thing?" (9:14).

One of the victims of this psychology of conformity, or, to use the musical term, "unison," is Lara's husband, Pasha Antipov. When he enters Yuryatin as the commander of a punitive detachment he declines to see his family since the balance of these two different roles and phases of his life seems absurd to him. Such events must take place only in linear sequence: "Suppose his wife and daughter were still there! Couldn't he go to them? Why not now, this very minute? Yes, but how could he? They belonged to another life. First he must see this one through, this new life, then he could go back to the one that had been interrupted. Someday he would do it. Someday. But when, when?" (7:31).

It stands to reason that the protagonist of the novel is in this respect the polar opposite of Antipov, and here is the root of the habitual "inactivity" and "weak will" of which he is accused by people with a limited, rationalistic view of life (for example, Antipov, Tonya, Gordon, and Dudorov) as well as his obvious deviations from moral convention. Zhivago's "two loves" are superimposed one on the other, the one neither reversing nor replacing the another. Much like his inner monologues, his study of medicine and poetry, his poems and prose writing concur rather than alternate: "Had he been unfaithful because he preferred another woman? No, he had made no comparison, no choice" (9:16).

Paradoxically, with a logic accessible to contrapuntal thinking, it is precisely the idea of "choice" in this situation, the acceptance of a conventional "resolution," that seems "vulgar" to Zhivago. His inability to choose some one path imparts a certain sense of hopelessness to his life. But the resolution of life's "counterpoints" is contained in their own nature. The conflict between life's various possibilities eventually leads them to reconcile themselves in the same "unforeseen" way, just as earlier they had been gathered into a knot that seemed irresolvable: "'What next?' he had sometime wondered, and hoped wretchedly for some impossible, unexpected circumstance to solve his problem for him" (9:16).

The proverb "Living life is not the same as crossing a field," with which the first of Zhivago's poems, "Hamlet," ends, gives aphoristic expression to this philosophy. At first glance, both the content of the proverb and its somewhat "folksy" style introduce an unpleasant dissonance into this profoundly serious philosophical poem. This stylistic juxtaposition, however, is characteristic of the philosophy and poetics of the novel: it highlights the literal meaning of the proverb: "crossing a field"; that is, taking a direct route moving in a linear fashion. In that poem the image of a thousand stars, the eyes of the audience trained on the poet, serve as the antithesis to this idea, the embodiment of contrapuntal, unhomogenized unity: "Night and its murk transfix and pin me, / Staring through thousands of binoculars" (17:1).

The scene of the Zhivago family's approach to Yuryatin in part 8 offers a similar antithesis in the actual narrative. In this scene Pasternak's favorite image of a brief halt along the railroad is juxtaposed to the image of the "open field" that the train cannot cross because of the endless "contrapuntal" switching of cars. That the delay was "foretold" by Tonya brings the whole situation even closer to "Hamlet" and lends it the character of a foreseen "order of the acts": "Antonina Aleksandrovna was right. Cars were coupled and uncoupled, and the train was shifted endlessly from one congested line to another where other trains blocked its way into the open country" (8:4).

One final level on which the principle of contrapuntal construction emerges is that of the novel's principal philosophical theme: the teleological idea of history developed by Zhivago and his spiritual mentor and "predecessor" Vedenyapin. Here the most important, truly great events, both in history and in art, enter into the flow of life without waiting for "the ground to be cleared" for them: they enter, we might say, the way a new voice enters into a polyphonic musical composition. Zhivago pictures the beginning of the revolution in precisely this way, as a symbolic image interlaced the characteristic "streetcars running throughout the city":

> And the real stroke of genius is this. If you charged someone with the task of creating a new world, of starting a new era, he would ask you first to clear the ground. He would wait for the old centuries to finish before undertaking to build the new ones, he'd want to begin a new paragraph, a new page.
>
> But here, they don't bother with anything like that. This new thing, this marvel of history, this revelation, is exploded right into the very thick of daily life without the slightest consideration for its course. It doesn't start at the beginning, it starts in the middle, without any schedule, on the first weekday that comes along, while the traffic in the street is at its height. That's real genius. Only real greatness can be so unconcerned with timing and opportunity. (6:8)

In Yury's view, the tragedy of the revolution lies in the loss of this polyphonic spontaneity, in the predominance of thinking characteristic of Antipov who strives first and foremost to "clear the ground" and to build both his own life and the course of history as a linear sequence, a goal that seems to him entirely possible and "thinkable."

For Zhivago and his teacher, the absolute and eternal example of the "greatest" is Christianity, the polyphonic "role" of which is one of the central tenets of the philosophy that Vedenyapin develops at the beginning of the novel: "And then, into this tasteless heap of gold and marble, He came, light and clothed in an aura, emphatically human, deliberately provincial, Galilean, and at that moment gods and nations ceased to be and man came into being – man the carpenter, man the plowman, man the shepherd with his flock of sheep at sunset, man who does not sound in the least proud, man thankfully celebrated in all the cradle songs of mothers and in all the picture galleries the world over" (2:10). The poetic image of this strikingly pedestrian, almost vulgar provinciality is drawn in Zhivago's poem "Star of the Nativity." Here "Galilean" provinciality is put into the context of the tradition of Russian folklore and popular culture.

Let us sum up Pasternak's artistic philosophy as it is expressed by his main characters. The polyphonic, nonlinear nature of everything "great" makes the moment of its appearance "irrelevant and inopportune." The truly great appears neither as a recurrence of what has happened before, nor as a loudly declared upheaval that demands a nihilistic "clearing of the ground." The great submits to nothing but also contradicts nothing. It is precisely because of this lack of delineation that what is "great" is not recognizable at first. The full approval or complete hostility, with which people confront everything clearly "old" or clearly "new," gives way to *confusion*, a feeling of awkwardness and "inappropriateness," shared by both supporters and opponents. For a clear vision, formed either by the existing order of things or by efforts to destroy that order, such a phenomenon inevitably seems at the moment of its emergence to be "out of focus" and creates the impression of something uneven, unfinished, and "provincial." A mind used to searching for the inner logic of even the most haphazard things turns out to be incapable of accepting this "provincial" inconsistency with respect to any conceivable aesthetic system or anti-system, this tangential relation to any projected intellectual, social, or aesthetic goal. Innovation of this scope "sounds not in the least bit proud" because it does not demand for itself a well-defined place. After all, the very idea of such a place along the lines of material historical progress is the antipode to contrapuntal thinking.

———

In the previous section we examined the fundamental principle in the construction of *Doctor Zhivago*'s narrative, illustrating this principle with the most characteristic but nonetheless isolated examples. The next step in our analysis is to demonstrate how contrapuntal lines interact with one another in the course of their development and how the novel's fabric as a whole is woven from the endless interlacing of these lines.[16]

It must be noted that in a work of such sophistication there is such an abundance of interconnections between various parts of the text, proceeding in different directions and based on a variety of shared features, that in the final analysis every distinguishable element of the narration appears to be connected, in one way or another, to be linked to every other element in this truly organic artistic whole. To give a complete analysis of such a matrix would be impossible and is hardly necessary. We will limit ourselves here to outlining a few of the novel's major thematic configurations, each of which can be easily supplemented and developed by turning to other points in the novel and, ultimately, to others of Pasternak's works.

The contrapuntal texture of the novel is created by interweaving various thematic and figurative lines that first join in the most improbable combinations at one point in the narrative, only to draw away from one another. Sometimes such combinations seem accessible to the characters, appearing to them simply as "improbable" coincidences. Sometimes these coincidences are communicated directly to the reader, who in turn may be perplexed about the excessive number of coincidences: "The man who had just died was Private Gimazetdin; the excited officer who had been shouting in the wood was his son, Lieutenant Galiullin; the nurse was Lara. Gordon and Zhivago were the witnesses. All these people were there together, in one place. But some of them had never known each other, while others failed to recognize each other now. And there were things about them which were never to be known for certain, while others were not to be revealed until a future time, a later meeting" (4:10).

It is also often true that the reader is not explicitly told, and therefore may not be aware of the "crossing of fates" that occurs in the novel. Only by juxtaposing different clues scattered throughout, the reader comes to realize a contrapuntal concurrence in what at first glance appears to be a commonplace situation or another "improbable" coincidence.

One such example is the seemingly unimportant episode of moving the wardrobe in the Gromekos' apartment, a small matter, to be sure, but one that leads to Anna Ivanovna's accidental fall resulting in prolonged illness (3:1). One result of this episode, the illness and death of Anna Ivanovna, is obvious. Another result is soon to follow: on her deathbed Anna Ivanovna asks Yury to marry Tonya. In this way one of the developmental lines that leads to the hero's marriage evolves from the episode with the wardrobe. Yet another far more distant connection is revealed if we turn our attention to the characters involved in this scene: "Markel, the porter, came to put it together. He brought with him his six-year-old daughter Marinka. She was given a stick of barley sugar. Sniffling, and sucking the candy and her moist fingers, she stood intently watching her father" (3:1). Marina is Zhivago's last wife, and the first "crossing" of her fate with his takes place in the episode with the wardrobe. Moreover, while assembling the wardrobe, Markel talks about unequal marriages and how in his youth he had passed up an opportunity to marry a "rich bride." He compares a bride from the upper classes with all the expensive furniture that "has passed through his hands." Thus we see that the series of associations of the wardrobe with the death of the foster mother and with marriage leads not only to Zhivago's first marriage, but also to his last.

The ominous role of the "wardrobe of black wood" seems obvious and even excessively straightforward: the word "wardrobe" (*garderob*) itself clearly recalls the word "coffin" (*grob*), and Anna Ivanovna nicknames the wardrobe the "tomb of Askold." It seems, however, that Anna Ivanovna actually had something else in mind: "She meant the horse of Prince Oleg, which had caused its master's death. She had read a great deal, but haphazardly, and she tended to confuse related ideas" (3:1). This true name remains only in the subconsciousness of Anna Ivanovna and is replaced in her consciousness by a nickname that belies a more trivially obvious and, in essence, false interpretation. According to the logic of this unarticulated, but true nickname, the wardrobe, the fall from which leads to Anna Ivanovna's death, turns out to be a "steed." By association this image is linked to two marginal points of the narrative: the death of Zhivago's father who throws himself from an express train, and the death of Zhivago himself after he jumps out of a streetcar. The more intently the reader studies the movement of this figurative fabric, the more it divulges unexpected confluences in the most conventional situations and turning points in the plot. From another point of view it reveals the inner logic in what at first glance appears to be naive coincidence, a clumsily placed seam in the design of the epic narrative.

Now we turn to yet another more complex chain of episodes that extends throughout the novel and serves as a graphic illustration of contrapuntal interweaving.

Episode 1 (1:2). The night after the funeral of Yury's mother a snowstorm breaks loose: "During the night the boy, Yura, was wakened by a knocking at the window. The dark cell was mysteriously lit up by a flickering whiteness. With nothing on but his shirt, he ran to the window and pressed his face against the cold glass" (1:2). The knocking reminds Yury of his dead mother and gives rise to the impulsive "desire to dress and run outside to begin doing something." The epithet "mysterious" suggests the mystical character of the situation. Two details of place and time add to the mystical cast. The action takes place in the monastery where Yury and his uncle, the priest "Father Nikolai" Vedenyapin, spend the night. The precisely noted time of the action is the "Eve of the Feast of the Intercession," that is, the holiday of the Intercession of the Holy Virgin. It is significant that the origin of this holiday is connected with the vision of *Andrei Yurodivy* (Andrei the Holy Fool, tenth century) to whom the Virgin appeared in a church as she extended her robe over the praying churchgoers. In this scene the vision of the snow as a "white cloth" covering the earth appears in the cell of a monastery to Yury *Andreevich* Zhivago.

The possibility of a mystical interpretation does not escape "Father Nikolai" whose reaction is described in the following way: "His uncle awoke, spoke to him about Christ, and consoled him, and then he yawned, walked to the window, and became lost in thought" (1:2). The reader can only conjecture as to the nature of Vedenyapin's reflections. Nothing is said directly about them, but, as is so often the case in this novel, a possible deeper meaning recedes into the background while the trivial, everyday gesture of yawning is highlighted.

Episode 2 (1:6). Several months later, Yura is praying for his dead mother: "Suddenly he remembered that he had not prayed for his missing father. . . . He thought that nothing terrible would happen if he prayed for his father some other time, as if saying to himself, 'Let him wait.' Yura did not remember him at all" (1:6). That Yura "forgot" his father is mentioned twice. Meanwhile, just at this moment of remembering his mother, his father commits suicide by throwing himself from a train. Significantly the suicide occurs *exactly* at the moment when Yura "suddenly" remembers that he had not prayed for his father.

Episode 3 (5:8–9). It is the eve of Lara's return home from the front. Her final conversation with Zhivago is marked by a contrast between surface simplicity, indeed, triviality, and hidden tension. A pedestrian detail serves as the background for the conversation: Lara is ironing laundry, steam is rising from the iron, and at the most dramatic point in the conversation the smell of something burning reaches them – she has forgotten about the iron and "burned a hole in a blouse." This detail stands out in all its unpleasant and possibly excessive banality. Annoyed, Lara sets the iron down on the stand "with a thump," thus marking with this gesture her resolution to break off the conversation and part – as they believe, forever.

After Lara's departure, Zhivago remains with Mademoiselle Fleury in the empty house. During the night they are both awakened by a persistent knock on the front door. Both think that Lara has returned, and both are disappointed when there is no one at the door. Again the "commonplace" imposes itself on the reader. As the doctor articulates it: "on this side, look, there's a broken shutter knocking on the casement, do you see it? That's all it was" (5:9). Once again no clear associative connection occurs to the doctor. All is left hidden in plain view, in the form of seemingly isolated, trivial details. However, a comparison with the opening scene of the novel shows that the knock at the door during a storm is in both episodes. Clearly the knock is a mystical gesture signaling death. It should also be noted that the knock of an unseen traveler typically represents a visit by the *angel of death*. The answer to the question as whom of the two residents of this house the angel of death was visiting will be given, to protagonist and reader alike, at the end of the novel when Zhivago and Fleury again meet at the "Hippodrome of Life."

Episode 4 (8:4). The Zhivago family is approaching Yuryatin. At the halt before the city, when the train "moved endlessly back and forth along the beaten tracks" (8:4), the entrepreneur Samdevyatov joins the travelers and tells the doctor about the inhabitants and sights of Yuryatin. Their conversation is made more difficult by the noise of the traincar wheels, so loud that every now and then the thread of their conversation is lost; they have to speak by "over-straining themselves from shouting." Among the details of the urban panorama unfolding before them is the billboard, "Moreau & Vet-chinkin. Mechanical Seeders. Threshing Machines." The advertised machines further advance the idea of clatter, that is, a kind of "knocking," and the French name "Moreau" can be associated with Mademoiselle Fleury, as well as with the idea of a "memento mori" (reminder of death). The surface of Zhivago's conversation with Samdevyatov gives no hint of these potential associations – just as it does not betray Zhivago's awareness that Antipova is very likely living in Yuryatin. Incidentally, Zhivago informs his interlocutor that they are preparing to live "not in the city," to which Samdevyatov rejoins that the doctor will certainly be visiting the city "on business." Among the sights worth visiting he mentions the city library. After Samdevyatov leaves at the next stop, the pragmatic Tonya, who is thinking only of the potential usefulness of Samdevyatov to the doctor's family, pronounces the incongruously solemn phrase, "In my opinion that man is sent to us by fate," to which Zhivago offers the totally meaningless reply: "Very possible, Tonechka" (8:6). The true meaning of this reply comes to light only later through recurring leitmotifs.

Episode 5 (9:5). The doctor is ill with a cough and shortness of breath. These symptoms bring him by some hidden logic to one of his "prophetic" diagnoses: he discovers in himself the first signs of the same hereditary heart ailment that carried off his mother. He realizes that he will eventually die of the same disease. This diagnosis looks especially illogical since he finds an immediate, simple explanation for what seems hardly more serious than a cold: Tonya is ironing, and the room is filled with a "slight charcoal smell" from the coal in the iron and from the clothes that are already ironed; in addition, a knock is heard – the "clank" of the lid of the iron. This picture "reminds" the protagonist of something: "I can't think what. Must be my condition." Then and there, however, the doctor recalls that Samdevyatov had brought them some soap, the reason for all the domestic activity. This recollection calls forth the sudden urge to go to the city, and, more precisely, to the library. The following night the doctor has a "confused dream," of which he remembers only the sound of a woman's voice that awakened him, but again he cannot remember whose voice it was. For us, it is well to keep in mind that a call in a dream is yet another classical image of the "angel of death."

On the surface this entire episode looks like a chain of rather simple, everyday associations: a cough and wheezing (the smell of charcoal as its immediate cause), the smell brought on by washing and ironing made possible by soap brought by Samdevyatov (the clank of the iron), the decision to go to the Yuryatin library, mentioned by Samdevyatov. Against the background of these banalities the premonition of death and the dream that foretells his meeting with Lara seem unexpected and unmotivated. Here we find yet another case of a "surprising" coincidence serving as the mainspring of the plot. However, after tracing the source of the images that come together in this episode and where they will lead, we can uncover the hidden meaning that looms behind this accumulation of commonplace events and melodramatic encounters and sudden insights. The "motif of the iron" and the "motif of the knock" permit association with the episodes of the death of Yury's mother and his earlier parting with Lara. The juxtaposition of these episodes in turn calls up an association with the "angel of death." In the light of such subliminal associations the thought of possibly bumping into Lara (who would be very likely to visit the city library) occurs to the doctor. Still this is a thought that the doctor blocks not only from his conversation, but also from the surface of his consciousness. Finally, in this context the observation that Samdevyatov was "sent by fate" acquires new meaning, although, of course, its initial, commonplace meaning receives full confirmation in the practical help that he offers to Zhivago and his family.

All these associations arise in the doctor's subconscious: hence his dream and his attempts to recall an elusive thought. The dream and efforts to recall prove to be a hidden force that channels Yury's feelings and behavior, giving a subliminal meaning to what at first appears trivial or melodramatically irrational. At the conclusion of this episode Zhivago himself articulates this principle of the interaction of the trivial and the profound: "Often it's something you paid no attention to at the time – a vague thought that you didn't bother to think out to the end, words spoken without feeling and which passed unnoticed – these are the things that return at night, clothed in flesh and blood, and they become the subjects of dreams, as if to make up for having been ignored during waking hours" (9:5). It is essential to note that Zhivago has described here a central principle of the poetics of the novel.

Episode 6 (9:10–12). The meeting of Zhivago and Antipova in the library. Here the web of leitmotifs from the two previous episodes, gathered together in the associative memory of both the protagonist and the reader, comes forth, bringing Zhivago to a series of successive "revelations" and "insights," that, in turn, connect together a still greater number of disparate details. As he sits in the library, Zhivago mulls over his memories of his first conversation with Samdevyatov and his first view of Yuryatin from the train, trying somehow to bring them into line with his current feelings. At first the doctor finds the simplest explanation for the association that has suddenly arisen in his mind: he recognizes one of the librarians as one of the Tuntseva sisters whom Samdevyatov had mentioned on the train. The characteristic trait by which Zhivago identifies her – the constant "sneezing" – corresponds with the "cough" of the doctor himself in the previous episode, the hidden spring of which were his thoughts about Lara Antipova. Only after this does Zhivago notice that Antipova has entered the reading room. He then realizes that the voice he had heard in his dream was hers. And finally, after meeting with Lara and visiting her home, the doctor discovers that from the window in her room one can see the same billboard he had seen from the train: "Moreau & Vetchinkin. Mechanical Seeders. Threshing Machines." This appears as a purely superficial coincidence, but its meaning can be exposed through a chain of deep mnemonic associations. At this moment Zhivago finally understands that the idea of meeting with Lara (whose whereabouts he had subliminally tried to detect by examining the buildings in the cityscape as it unfolded before him on his arrival) and the "reminder of death" were connected in his mind from the very first moment of his arrival in Yuryatin.

Episode 7 (15:12). The last episode in the chain is marked by the death of the hero. We have already examined the fundamental components on which this scene is built; now we are in a position to come to a fuller understanding of each of these components and how they interact.

As he rides in the streetcar, Zhivago observes an old woman walking along the sidewalk, periodically appearing and then disappearing from view. Since he does not consciously recognize her as Mademoiselle Fleury, he is incapable of interpreting the symbolic detail of her attire: a hat "with linen daisies and cornflowers" that metonymically represent her name. As with the other cases we have examined, this detail, which will remain buried in Yury's subconscious, unleashes in him a chain of subliminal associations resulting in thoughts and actions, the logic of which can be understood only by taking into account all the associative clues from previous episodes.

The meeting with Mademoiselle Fleury is first and foremost a reminder of the visit of the "angel of death." This reminder is intensified by the knocking motif (here, the clank of the streetcar's wheels and the crack of a short circuit that time and again puts the streetcar out of service), by the impending storm, and finally by the doctor's sickness and the irregular beating of his heart. This hidden associative setting calls to the surface thoughts about death and the image of a "hippodrome" (*ristalishche*) in which people compete for survival, "who will outlive whom." It is now time to settle the question as to which of the two had received the death "warrant" in episode 2. In this fatal reckoning the excessively old age of Mademoiselle Fleury mentioned several times in this scene is weighed against the unhealthy heart of the doctor.

The thought of death is finally firmly linked in Yury's consciousness to the death of his mother: he had foreseen some time ago that he would die of the same heart ailment as his mother had. What is more, after the heart attack started, his desperate attempts first to open the window, and then to escape from the streetcar, are associated to his behavior the night after the death of his mother (compare with episode 1), when he peered intensely through the window ("pressed his face to the cold glass") and felt an overwhelming desire to run outside and "to do something." At the same time, however, it becomes clear that Zhivago essentially reenacts the death of his father: he impulsively jumps from the streetcar and dies, thus accomplishing the same symbolic act of abandoning "life's journey" that his father did when he threw himself from the express train. Thus, behind the connection of his death from a heart attack with his mother's death (obvious to both Zhivago and the reader), another, deeper connection is illuminated: the link between his own death and that of his father.

At the moment of his father's death Zhivago had forgotten about him and thought only about his deceased mother. This circumstance can be interpreted as a mystical reason contributing to his father's suicide. Later, in his anticipation of his own death, the doctor again thinks only of his mother, and again fails to remember his father.

Zhivago's actions in the streetcar can be construed in such a way that at the last moment he realizes that again, for the second time in his life he has made a mistake by forgetting his father, and this mistake had led him to misinterpret the news he had received from the "angel of death." The true meaning of this news was that his own death would be a repetition of the death of his father. Apparently Zhivago had guessed a long time ago the mystical significance of the sound of the knock as a detail linked to his death. However, his interpretations of that motif had been wrong or, at least, incomplete: he had thought that it signified an arrhythmic beating of his weak heart. Only at the last moment does he understand that his death is to occur amidst the clatter of a "train" (this time, a streetcar), a clue given to him, of which he is still unconscious on the day of his arrival in Yuryatin, when he listened to the clank of the wheels of the train and looked at the "memento mori" advertisement, "Moreau & Vetchinkin."

The novel is so thoroughly saturated with details and their simple, commonplace interpretations; so openly and naively does the author time and again confess to resorting in his narrative to all kinds of chances, coincidences, and irrational actions on the part of his characters, that the driving force of the narrative remains veiled. I have in mind the interwoven contrapuntal lines linking the evolution of events and the spiritual development of the characters. Explanations referring to a contrapuntal intertwining of the characters' fates and thought are rarely offered to the reader in a direct and open form; in any case, they are not offered at those moments when the reader might reasonably expect them. Readers themselves must understand the meaning of that "silent" information that the novel carries in itself. They must find where the threads unite and decipher the whole picture suggested by these juxtapositions. This kind of interpretation can never be expressed in a definitive and fixed form: it will always necessarily have a hypothetical and ambiguous character.

For example, the chains of Yury's thoughts and actions described above can be explained psychologically as a pattern of subconscious memory at work. And a poetic-mythological interpretation could carry equal interpretive force through an examination of the same clues as elements of the biographical myth of the poet; that is, as the result of his associative artistic thinking that intuitively assembles all received impressions into an artistic picture of the world with its own internal poetic logic.[17] After all, Zhivago is a poet, and one might expect that this side of his personality would emerge in the novel in more than the few episodes in which he is shown discussing poetry and writing poems, but in the whole rhythm of his life. Still another explanation, no less logical in itself and no less essential from the point of view of the ideas developed in the novel, could illuminate the novel by interpreting the events described in it as acts of mystical revelation. Finally, the novel's logic may be interpreted as the logic of a pantheistic world order, in which every part of existence reso-nates in the endless spheres of cosmic harmony: an interpretation in which Pythagorean and Platonic mysticism could be linked to twentieth-century achievements in mathematics and physics, as, for example, the theory of relativity.

Of course, along with all these "prestigious" interpretations there is still one more that "sounds not in the least bit proud." There is nothing irrational or illogical about the narrative of *Doctor Zhivago* if we view it as an example of a "popular" potboiler about love, jeal-ousy, death, meetings, separations, suicides, deadly villains, proph-ecies, premonitions, secret signs sent from the other world – all this set against a noble background of dramatic, historical events and accompanied by, to borrow Nabokov's ironic phrase, "unnatural snowstorms." The strength of the novel lies precisely in this indeter-minacy and openness to a variety of equally possible interpretations.

When Gordon and Dudorov accuse Zhivago of letting himself go, of losing connection with people and life, and of isolating himself in "unwarranted arrogance," the protagonist either keeps silent or gets away with empty, pathetically trite answers that, it would seem, graphically confirm his accusers' point: "I think everything will come out all right. . . . You'll see. I really mean it. . . . in any case, you must let me go" (15:7). Only an attentive look at the fabric of motifs behind this off-putting mask reveals the traces of intense spiritual work that Gordon and Dudorov, who mistake the external for the essential, cannot see. Only occasionally do the results of this work break through to the surface with full force in Zhivago's insights, his creative work, and his impulsive actions: in those manifestations of his personality that make a deep impression on those around him but that are perceived as unexpected and unexplicable outbursts. In this respect, the character of the protagonist fully corresponds to the character of the novel itself: like its hero, the novel leaves unanswered all claims and confusions that the reader may experience, allowing the reader to guess at the inner meaning of the interwoven threads hidden behind its abundance of eclectic and quite often banal details, conversations, and plot situations.

NOTES

1. A. Gladkov, author of some wonderful memoirs on Pasternak, expressed well the reaction to the novel of the reader who has been immersed in the world of Pasternak's lyrics: "In *Doctor Zhivago* there are marvelous pages, but there would be more of them if the author had not made an effort to write a *novel*. . . . Everything that is novelistic in this book is weak: characters don't speak or act without prompting from the author. All the conversations of characters who are intellectuals are either naive personifications of the author's thoughts, clumsily masked behind dialogue or artless imitation. All the crowd scenes seem almost false because of their language" (Aleksander Gladkov, *Vstrechi s Pasternakom* [Paris: YMCA Press, 1973], 137).

2. V. Erlich accurately articulated this approach, which received wide dissemination in critical literature about the novel: "It is, perhaps, the crowning paradox of Pasternak's paradox-ridden career that this one 'epic' of his should have been in a sense more personal and autobiographical than are many of his lyrics"; Victor Erlich, introduction to *Pasternak: A Collection of Critical Essays*, ed. V. Erlich (Englewood Cliffs, N.J.: Prentice-Hall, 1978), 8. Supporters of this point of view quite often specially emphasize the wrongness of comparing *Doctor Zhivago* with the epic novel tradition and, in particular, with the national epic of Tolstoy; see, for example, Henry Gifford, *Pasternak: A Critical Study* (Cambridge: Cambridge University Press, 1977), 182.

3. Czeslaw Milosz, "On Pasternak Soberly," *Books Abroad* 44, no. 2 (1970): 200–208.

4. An example of the fullest and most rigorous interpretation of *Doctor Zhivago* as an allegory of the Apocalypse is a book entirely devoted to this topic: Mary F. Rowland and Paul Rowland, *Pasternak's 'Doctor Zhivago'* (Carbondale: Southern Illinois University Press, 1967).

5. Intentions of writing a novel that would sum up his entire creative career, a novel that would show "all of life" are repeated throughout Pasternak's correspondence and documented oral conversations from the end of the 1940s and the beginning of the 1950s. One example: on July 9, 1952, Pasternak wrote to V. T. Shalamov about his need to make the transition from what he dismissively called "writing verse" to a new, more significant and "real" job: "from all these innumerable failures and things said in the wrong words [*nedomolvka*] . . . I must forge ahead and step across to a world that will give me a unifying idea for all these trivial attempts; I need to do something in life; I need to write a story about life that brings out something new about life, a discovery or a conquest; I need to build a house for which all this poorly written verse can be the window frames" "'Razgovory o samom glavnom': Perepiska B. L. Pasternaka i V. T. Shalamova," *Iunost'* 10 (1988), 55.

6. See in particular the work of Barnes, which contains the publication of one of Pasternak's musical compositions: Christopher J. Barnes, "Boris Pasternak: The Musician-Poet and Composer," *Slavica Hierosolymitana* 1 (1976): 317–35.

7. Krystyna Pomorska's work is of particular importance for an understanding of the role of music in the lyrics of Pasternak; an especially important investigation is her *Themes and Variations in Pasternak's Poetics* (Lisse: Peter de Ridder Press, 1975), chap. 2 ("Music as Theme and Structure").

8. In all references to the text of *Doctor Zhivago* the numbers in parentheses indicate, correspondingly, the section and chapter of the novel. English citations are taken from *Doctor Zhivago*, trans. M. Hayward and M. Harari (New York: Ballantine, 1981).

9. See in particular: K. Pomorska, *Themes and Variations*, 74–75.

10. Aldous Huxley, *Point Counter Point* (New York: Harper and Row, 1965), 301.

11. See Birnbaum's full-scale comparison of *Doctor Zhivago* and *Doctor Faust* in which he examines, in particular, the role of a musical theme in both

novels: Henrik Birnbaum, *Doktor Faustus und Doktor Schiwago. Versuch über zwei Zeitromane aus Exilsicht* (Lisse: Peter de Ridder Press, 1976).

12. See *Safe Conduct* and *Autobiographical Sketch*, as well as "Letters from Tula."

13. For a detailed analysis of this image in ancient Slavic mythology, see V. V. Ivanov and V. N. Toporov, *Issledovaniia v oblasti slavinskikh drevnostei* (Moscow: Nauka, 1974), 86–125; see also A. N. Afanas'ev, *Poeticheskie vozzreniia slavian na prirodu* (Moscow: n.p., 1865), 1:252–56.

14. Interesting observations on the meaning of liturgical time in the development of the action of the novel can be found in Dimitrii Obolenskii, "Stikhi doktora Zhivago," in *Sbornik statei posviashchennykh tvorchestvu Borisa Leonidovicha Pasternaka* (Munich, 1962), 103–14.

15. Compare the investigation of "dualism" in the language of *Doctor Zhivago* in L. Rzhevskii, "Iazyk i stil' romana B. L. Pasternaka *Doktor Zhivago*," in *Sbornik statei posviashchennykh tvorchestvu Borisa Leonidovicha Pasternaka* (Munich: Institut zur Erforschung der UdSSR, 1962), 184–86.

16. The positive structural role of coincidences on which the composition of the novel is built was first shown by Struve: Gleb Struve, "The Hippodrome of Life: The Problem of Coincidence in *Doctor Zhivago*," *Books Abroad* 44, no. 2 (1970): 231–36.

17. This concept was introduced by Roman Jakobson in his classic article about Pushkin's statue myth: "Socha v symbolice Puskinove," *Slovo a slovesnost* 3 (1937): 2–24. For further discussion of this problem, and, in particular, its connections with the life and creative work of Pasternak, see Roman Jakobson and Krystyna Pomorska, *Besedy* (Jerusalem: Magnes Press, 1982), chap. 14.

The Relationship of Lyrical and Narrative "Plot" in *Doctor Zhivago*

DINA MAGOMEDOVA

To begin with the obvious: *Doctor Zhivago* ends with a remarkable cycle of poetry. The author Pasternak gave his hero Yury Zhivago his own best poems, thereby revealing the novel's deeply autobiographical character. These poems illustrate less the facts of the "external" biographies of author and protagonist, which do not really converge, than aspects of shared creative experience. In their own way, the poems from the novel are the highest justification of the protagonist's life. Depending on one's point of view, moving either from the narrative to the cycle or from the cycle to the novel, the aesthetic function of the prosaic and poetic parts of the novel can seem to shift: the poems may be perceived as a creative transformation and rethinking of prosaic actuality, while individual episodes from the novel may be seen as a kind of commentary to the poems.

Several poems, for example, "Bad Roads in Spring," "Autumn," "Parting," or "Encounter," are directly connected to specific scenes from the prose narrative. The creative history of other poems, for example, "Winter Night," is given in the narrative text. Yet another group of poems builds on evangelical themes. Among these are "Hamlet," "Holy Week," "August," "Star of the Nativity," "Miracle," "Evil Days," "Magdalene," and "Garden of Gethsemane." These poems lend mythic depth to the events of the novel.

Clearly, by juxtaposing narrative and lyric segments of *Doctor Zhivago*, we can find the key to some specific characteristics of Pasternak's creative process and aesthetic views. Although this essay can only provide an outline to both of these questions, I hope that it will open the way for more detailed examination and elaboration. It is also true, incidentally, that in talking about *Doctor Zhivago* we will be examining an interaction between lyrical and narrative discourse that was also characteristic of much of Pasternak's other work.

What does this repetition of setting in both lyrical and narrative parts mean? Clearly, we may assume that there resides in the writer's creative consciousness a certain orientation to plot that allows for the most diverse structural formations: from fully developed ("linear") plot narrative to the reproduction of specific "points" (to use Iurii Lotman's term) or fragments of narrative plot in lyric verse. In other words, this single plot-related "constant" is realized in Pasternak's work in a number of generic "variants," sometimes clearly, sometimes only indirectly connected among themselves. We must allow for the coexistence of several "variants" of one plot when we examine the creative history of any Pasternak text. At the same time, the "point" type of plot used in lyric verse, that reproduces only a piece of an event, can prove to be the connecting link between two works that at first glance seem quite unrelated. A good example of this interaction is offered by the poem "Autumn" from the Zhivago cycle that is linked in important ways to the narrative plot of the novel:[1]

> I have let all the members of my household go their ways;
> All those close to me have long since scattered.
> And everything – within the heart and throughout nature –
> Is filled with the loneliness of always.
>
> And now I am here with you in the forester's hut.
> The forest is unpeopled and deserted.
> Its trails and paths are (as the old song has it)
> Half overgrown with grass and weeds.
>
> We are the only ones now
> For the walls of logs to regard in melancholy.
> We made no promises to storm barricades;
> We shall go down to perdition openly.

We will take our seats at one; at three we will leave our seats –
I with a book, you with your needlework.
And when day breaks we shall not notice
And what time we had done with our kissing.

Be noisy, leaves, as you flutter down –
Still more flamboyantly, with more abandon!
And raise the level of the gall of yesterday
Within the cup, by adding to it today's yearning.

Attachment, craving, splendor of beauty. . . .
Let us scatter like smoke in this September soughing.
Bury all of yourself, my dearest, in this autumnal rustling;
Swoon, or go half insane!

You shed your coverings in much the same fashion
As this grove sheds its leaves,
Whenever you fall into my embraces
In your dressing gown with its silken tassels.

You are the blessing in a stride toward perdition,
When living sickens more than sickness does itself;
The root of beauty is audacity,
And that is what draws us to each other.

Осень
Я дал разъехаться домашним,
Все близкие давно в разброде,
И одиночеством всегдашним
Полно все в сердце и природе.

И вот я здесь с тобой в сторожке,
В лесу безлюдно и пустынно.
Как в песне, стежки и дорожки
Позаросли наполовину.

Теперь на нас одних с печалью
Глядят бревенчатые стены.

Мы брать преград не обещали,
Мы будем гибнуть откровенно.

Мы сядем в час и встанем в третьем,
Я с книгою, ты с вышиваньем,
И на рассвете не заметим,
Как целоваться перестанем.

Еще пышней и бесшабашней
Шумите, осыпайтесь, листья,
И чашу горечи вчерашней
Сегоняшней тоской превысьте.

Привязанность, влеченье, прелесть!
Рассеемся в сентябрьском шуме!
Заройся вся в осенний шелест!
Замри, или ополоумей!

Ты так же сбрасываешь платье,
Как роща сбрасывает листья,
Когда ты падаешь в обьятье
В халате с шелковою кистью.

Ты—благо гибельного шага,
Когда житье тошней недуга,
А корень красоты—отвага,
И это тянет нас друг к другу.

The poem re-creates an episode from part 14 ("Return to Varykino") when Yury and Lara are found at the summer dacha after the departure of Yury's family to Moscow. It is equally certain that the plot of this poem also reaches back to the first and second chapters of Pasternak's earlier novel fragment, "The Beginning of the Prose Fragment from 1936" ("The Beginning of the Novel about Patrick"; see the Introduction for a discussion of "Patrick's Notes"). The setting is the same: two people stay behind at a dacha after the departure of the rest of the family. The themes of love and death are marked here as the fate that awaits the protagonists in the near future. In the second chapter the family of the protagonist must depart for Moscow from their summer estate in the Urals, while the heroine Evgenia Vikentievna Istomina, who had been visiting the dacha, may not legally return to the city and does not want to leave the dacha. Let us examine it:

"Have a talk with her," Aleksandr Aleksandrovich suggested. "Wouldn't it indeed be a good idea to take her with you to Moscow?"

I do not remember her answer, it seems to me that under these circumstances I may not have received any answer at all. Perhaps she said that she was intending to guard over the dacha – unless, of course, we were going to turn her out – but what kind of answer was this, this readiness to spend the winter alone with a child in a forest filled with the howling of wolves and swept by snowstorms? I wish that she had mentioned that she would not like to stay alone and that she would need to find someone to protect her.

I told Aleksandr Aleksandrovich about our conversation and said that they should go, and I would stay on a little while at the mill in order to finish writing an article. . . . After helping Evgenia Vikentievna find a place to stay in Yurytin, I would return home with the article finished – by my reckoning in November or, at the latest, the end of November.

There was no secret purpose here. Such were my true intentions. No one doubted me in this. But my relatives turned out to be the more far-sighted. They were greatly alarmed at my decision as if they already could see what would happen, and they started to dissuade me. The conversation ended with everyone in tears. But I didn't give in. We had to postpone their departure for a few days after which they finally left.[2]

The similarity between the lyric setting and the scene from the novel fragment requires no further comment. In both, the chronotopes (or setting in time and space) are the same: autumn, the forest, the lodge, and the description of the characters' moods. Compare the line from the poem: "We shall go down to perdition openly" to the following passage from the novel fragment: "Istomina was the only one of us with a clearly broken life. More than any other person she corresponded to my predilections of the end."[3] And a comparison of the episodes from *Doctor Zhivago* and "Patrick's Notes" also shows that the names of the protagonists' relatives are the same: the father-in-law, Aleksandr Aleksandrovich; the wife, Tonya; the son, Shura. The names of the protagonists themselves are new, which is to be expected.

The poem "Autumn" thus functions as the point of intersection between two narrative plots, of *Doctor Zhivago* and of "Patrick's Notes." The creative history of *Doctor Zhivago* begins almost in 1918 when, after his return from the Urals, Pasternak wrote a novel that was subsequently destroyed, the beginning of which turned into the story "The Childhood of Louvers." And, indeed, the heroine of "Patrick's Notes" is none other than the young Zhenia Louvers now grown up. Although *Doctor Zhivago* eventually lost its direct connection with the early prose fiction (as we can see from the change in the protagonists' names), the "plot" setting of the poem "Autumn" allows us to probe more deeply into the early stages of Pasternak's creative project. This correlation of the lyric and narrative plots is important for reasons other than the compilation of a "general list" of plot variants of a single storyline. The realization of a single plot in different genres is a way of transforming one and the same situation and bringing out its interpretive potential by inserting it into different "chains of signification."

Despite all the similarities between their settings it would be incorrect to say that the poem "Autumn," "Patrick's Notes," and *Doctor Zhivago* all share a common plot. The composition of the lyric poem is different from the linear narrative plot of the prose fiction. If we trace the internal logic of the plot of "Autumn," we will discover that it moves between two planes: the narrative, dealing with the everyday, clearly referring to episodes in the novel, and the folkloric, with its unexpected confluence of motifs central to the poem and the compositional structure of the well-known folktale of the "house in the forest."[4]

This duality of levels is apparent already in the first stanza. The lines "I have let all the members of my household go their ways / All those close to me have long since scattered" are naturally perceived as the start of a narrative from everyday life. At the same time these lines reiterate the motif of the "departure of one's intimates" (*otluchka blizkikh*) at the beginning of the folktale of the "house in the forest" (Propp, 36–37). The first stanza introduces the parallel between the levels of natural and human life, characteristic of the poetics of folklore ("And everything – within the heart and throughout nature – / Is filled with the loneliness of always").

We find the same two levels in the second stanza: the first couplet continues the narrative plot ("And now I am here with you in the forester's hut. / The forest is unpeopled and deserted") and simultaneously develops motifs from the folktale: the protagonists remain in the house alone after the departure of their intimates. Again the second couplet certainly refers to folkloric tradition through a quotation from a popular song ("Its trails and paths are (as the old song has it) / Half overgrown with grass and weeds").

The image of the forest resonates with both everyday and folkloric motifs. In the folktale plot the forest is the boundary between the realms of the living and the dead (Propp, 58). The goal of the folktale hero is to cross the boundary: either to enter the kingdom of the dead or to get out of it (Propp, 48, 56–57). In the third stanza of the poem the opportunity to follow the logic of the folktale plot is declined ("We made no promises to storm barricades; / We shall go down to perdition openly"). Thus what happens to the protagonists in the "forester's hut" is called "perdition." But the fourth stanza again returns the plot to the realm of everyday by drawing an almost idyllic family scene. At the same time this stanza also develops conjugal motifs – always characteristic for the tale of the "house in the forest" in which the hero often marries, sometimes for a second time, forgetting his first wife, or sometimes temporarily, lasting only in the kingdom of the dead (Propp, 131–33).

The fifth and sixth stanzas represent the climax of the folktale aspect of the plot. The verse loses its sense of narrative movement (grammatically this loss is expressed in the substitution of the imperative for the indicative mood of the verbs) and finds intonations typical of invocations. The drama of death is played out on the level of both the "natural" and "human." Death in nature is maximally humanized through anthropomorphizing epithets and predicates: "with more abandon" (*besshabashnei*), and "And raise the level of the gall of yesterday / Within the cup, by adding to it today's yearning" (*I chashu gorechi vcherashnei / Segodniashnei toskoi prevys'te*). The reuniting of the protagonists is intended to identify fully with death in nature ("Let us scatter like smoke in this September soughing. / Bury all of yourself, my dearest, in this autumnal rustling"). Of special significance is the line "Swoon, or go half insane!" The motifs of temporary death and temporary insanity form an essential part of the tale of the house in the forest; in one way or another they originate in ceremonies of initiation, of ordination during which the hero must die temporarily, leave the usual flux of life, and then return to life as a different person and enter into a new existence (Propp, 89–90). In the last two stanzas the characters experience a gradual return to everyday reality: the folkloric "language" of parallelism and identity gives way to an extended simile: "You shed your coverings in much the same fashion / As this grove sheds its leaves."[5] The final stanza is in its own way a poetical summary in which it is precisely the possibility for rebirth, for overcoming isolation that is revealed ("You are the blessing in a stride toward perdition").

Was Pasternak aware of the possibility of interpreting this poem through the prism of the folktale? An investigation into the creative history of the novel allows us to answer in the affirmative. V. M. Borisov and E. B. Pasternak note that while working on the novel Pasternak not only made "wide use of folkloric sources: collections of folklore from the Ural Mountains, *Russian Folk-Tales* by A. N. Afanasev, *The Malachite Box* by P. P. Bazhov, and personal notes on folk ways"; he also "was absorbed" by V. N. Propp's *The Historical Roots of the Fairy Tale*, which appeared in 1946. The authors quote a letter of Pasternak's from November 9, 1954, to T. M. Nekrasova that shows the intentional orientation of the novel to the poetics of the folktale: "Book One now seems to me like an introduction to the second, more unusual [book]. What makes it so unusual, it seems to me, is that I put reality, that is, the totality of events still farther from the conventional than in the first book, almost on the edge of a folktale" (Borisov and Pasternak, "Materialy," 242). The plot of "Autumn," thus, displays an internal logic that can be reduced to individual episodes in the novel, but still appeals to deeper layers of meaning in the novel as a whole, to the possibility for moral and spiritual rebirth in a catastrophically changing world.

In Pasternak's work in general the "point" type of plot of the lyric poem represents a transition from a cosmic, panoramic view of the world to a momentary penetration into the internal, spiritual world of the lyric self and then a return to the initial overarching view. At the same time the heart of the poem, in which other narrative plots echo, gains completely new meaning beside other parallel prose variants. In the "linear" narrative plot this single "point" or event is motivated by previous action; it has a definite, and, indeed, often only one possible outcome. In the context of the lyric poem, where all causal motivations and all "pre-histories" are arrested, this single moment is open to multiple interpretations, despite the illusion of the singularity and uniqueness of the setting. Thus the question of the correlation between narrative and lyric plot in Pasternak's art stands out as one of the central problems of his poetics: the problem of the generic transformation of shared qualities of plot formation and the problem of multiple transformations of events and situations initially existing in the everyday.

NOTES

This essay is an abridged version of an article that appeared under the same title in *Izvestiia Akademii Nauk SSSR: Seriia literatury i iazyka*, 5 (1990).

1. All citations are taken from the translation of *Doctor Zhivago* by Max Hayward and Manya Harari (New York: Ballantine, 1981).

2. Boris Pasternak, *Vozdushnye puti: Proza raznykh let* (Moscow, 1982), 290.

3. Ibid., 300.

4. The house in the forest is a setting essential to many Russian folk tales (and more than a few of Grimms' folk tales, such as "The Musicians of Bremen" or "Hansel and Gretel"). In Russian tales, for example, about the witch Baba Iaga, the house is a cottage or a hut that the hero, or sometimes both hero and heroine, visit in order to complete some task set for them. Here a kind of rite of initiation takes place. The hero leaves transformed by his experience. For more on this motif, see V. Ia. Propp, *Istoricheskie korni volshebnoi skazki* (Leningrad, 1986); hereafter cited in text as Propp.

5. For more about parallelism and comparison as two historical languages of poetry see A. P. Veselovskii, *Istoricheskaia poetika* (Leningrad, 1940), 189; S. N. Broitman, *Problema dialoga v russkoi lirike pervoi poloviny XIX veka* (Makhachkala, 1983), 6–9.

III  PRIMARY SOURCES

Correspondence
Relating to *Doctor Zhivago*

BETWEEN BORIS PASTERNAK AND OLGA FREIDENBERG[1]

Moscow, October 5, 1946
Dear Olya!

. . .

In July I began to write a novel in prose entitled "Boys and Girls," the ten chapters of which are meant to embrace four decades from 1902 to 1946, and, completely absorbed, I have finished a quarter or a fifth of what I had planned. These are all very serious labors. I am already old, and I may die soon, and I cannot put off forever saying freely what I really think. This year's projects are the first step on that journey, and they are extraordinary. You cannot go on at thirty, forty, and at fifty-six living on and on in the same way as an eight-year-old child lives: on mere potential and the good will of those around you – my whole life has passed according to this forcibly restrained plan.

At first all the "current events" did not touch my own life in the least little bit.[2] I sat in Peredelkino and worked enthusiastically on the third chapter of my epic. . . .

This whole past year I have been filled to overflowing with a feeling of happiness and the most lively belief in it. And before taking up my interrupted work (I decided to set to it again today), I wanted, while I have time, to give you news about us all. . . .

Your B.

Monday, October 13, 1946
Dear Olya!

On the very day I wrote to you I caught a nasty cold and was sick in bed for several days.

Now I am in a very bad mood, I'm in one of those long spells that have beset my life a number of times, but now this spell has combined with genuine old age, beside which over the last five years I have grown so accustomed to health and success that I had begun to consider happiness a constant and compulsory part of my existence.

In one regard I will try to take myself in hand – in my work. I already told you that I have begun a large novel in prose. In fact, it is my first genuine work. In it I want to give a historical image of Russia over the last forty-five years, and, at the same time, in all aspects of its plot – difficult, sad, and worked out in detail, ideally as in Dickens or Dostoevsky – this thing will be the expression of my views on art, the Gospels, human life in history, and many other things. For the time being I am calling the novel "Boys and Girls." In it I am settling accounts with Judaism [*evreistvo*], with all kinds of nationalism (including the kind apparent in internationalism), with all kinds of anti-Christianities and their assumptions – as if after the fall of the Roman empire there could really have existed genuine nations [*narody*] and they could really have formed a unique culture on the basis of some notion of essential national character.

The atmosphere of the thing will be my own Christianity, in its breadth it is somewhat different from Quakerism and Tolstoyanism, exploring several other aspects of the Gospel beside its ethical thought.

This is all so important and the color is so appropriate to my planned outlines that I will not last a year if this reincarnation of myself, into which, almost physically, pieces of viscera and nerve have been transplanted, does not live and grow over the next year. . . .

Your Borya

[Moscow,] October 1 [1948]
My Olyushka . . .

. . .

I am now translating the first part of Goethe's *Faust* with furious haste in order with this haste to earn the opportunity and the right to continue and perhaps in the winter even finish my novel, a completely unselfish and unprofitable undertaking, since the novel is not destined for publication under current conditions. And what is more, I am not writing it at all as a work of art, although it is fiction in a larger sense than my earlier things were. But I do not know whether there is any art left in the world and what meaning that might have. There are people who love me very much (there are very few of them), and my heart is in debt to them. For them I write this novel, I'm writing it as a long letter to them, in two books. I am glad that I carried the first through to the end. Would you like me to send you a copy of the manuscript for two weeks or a month? You will find it hard to take my oversimplified, caricature-like conceptualizations of antiquity (I put them there in order to make the essence of Christianity stand out in a more vivid and striking way).

Moscow, [mid-October, 1948]

. . .

I am sending this manuscript to you all. Read in whatever order you wish, but perhaps Olya could start, so that she will then write to me sooner. If possible, try not to have each person keep the manuscript for very long for I may soon need it back again.

Probably this, the first book, is written for, and for the sake of, the second which covers the period from 1917 until 1945. . . . In its plot and its central idea this second book is readier in my mind than the first book was at *its* conception, but in order for us to be able to live at all (after all, this prose is not intended for the time being for publication), I must work at translation, and consequently work on the novel had to be interrupted. Now in the hope that I may complete it before Christmas I am hastily translating Goethe's *Faust* (the first part) and a certain Hungarian classical poet. I am bursting with ideas and projects and I feel like working as never before.

After all, beside surviving the revolution, we have also lived through a time of general disintegration of the basic forms of consciousness, and all useful habits and ideas, all kinds of expedient skill, have been shaken.

One comes so late in life to a realization of what is indispensable that only now I grasped what I needed to do all along – what can I do, but I'm grateful at least for that.

But in case you are interested, I am really happy, not in some kind of exalted way or through some kind of paradoxical perspective on life, but in reality because I am inwardly free and at present, thanks to the Creator, healthy. I send you all a big kiss and love you very much.

Your Borya

Leningrad, November 29, 1948
My dear Borya!

Finally I got to read your novel. What do I think of it? I am at a loss: what do I think of life? This is life in its broadest and greatest sense. Your book is higher than judgment. What you say about history as a second universe is applicable to it [your book]. It breathes vastness. Its special quality is something special (an unexpected tautology), and it is not to be found in the genre or in the plot, and even less so in the characters. I can't put my finger on it, and I would like to hear what people say about it. It is a special version of the Book of Genesis. In it your genius is very deep. Its philosophical passages made my skin tingle: I was just afraid that at any moment a final mystery would be revealed, one that you carry within and your whole life have wanted to express, you have awaited its expression in art or science – and you're scared to death of its final expression because, to live on, it must remain an eternal riddle. You cannot imagine what kind of reader I am: I read the book, and you, and our common blood ties, and therefore my view is not an ordinary, accessible one. This work needs to be possessed completely and not simply read, as a woman is not read, but possessed. This kind of reading on the quick is almost absurd.

I am not interested in the book as realism in genre or language. It is not these things that I value. In the novel there is a grandeur of a different sort, almost unendurable in scale, more than its ideas. But, you know, *for me* the last impression, when I close the book, is terrifying. It seems to me that you fear death, and that this explains everything – your passionate immortality which you are creating as your most intimate achievement. In this I understand you completely: as a relative of yours I feel sad – some are no longer living, and those are beyond Tyutchev's "I await my fateful turn." It is the same feeling as when you descend into the metro: you stand in place, and suddenly you are at the bottom . . .

There is much here that is close to me, familiar, completely my own, something of our family's need for something grand, for the most important thing, right down to the articulation and resolution of personal problems. But by the familiar and the familial (as also by the fear of death) I understand the great as it is transposed into the private (but without turning into petty trifles). But do not talk nonsense, as if everything [you had written] before this were worthless, and that only now . . . etc. You are one whole, and your whole life's journey lies here, like a picture with a road that you can see leading into the deep distance. The poems you included are one with your prose and with your other poetry. And they are very good.

But what I'm writing isn't what I perceive. Instead of answering with a letter I should really answer with a long kiss. How I understand you in what is most important to you! . . .

Your Olya

Moscow, November 30, 1948
My dear Olyushka!

How striking your letter was!

Your letter is a thousand times better and greater than my manuscript. So that's how you saw it?! It is not so much a fear of death as a consciousness of the futility of the best intentions and achievements, and of the best assurances, and my consequent effort to avoid naïveté and take the right road, so that should something be lost, then at least that thing will be flawless, so that nothing should perish through my own mistake. Don't rack your brain over these words. If you do not understand them, so much the better.

You often mention blood ties, family. Imagine those as merely the proscenium in events that we have seen, merely the focal point for a whole drama that is basically more of the same. The main shock in my life was my father, his brilliance, his fantastic control over form, his eye, unparalleled among his contemporaries, the ease of his mastery, his ability playfully to sketch several pictures in a day, and the incongruously poor reception of his work, and then suddenly I felt it (the sense of shock) again with Tsvetaeva, who was extraordinarily talented, courageous, sophisticated, who experienced all the reversals of our "epic" time, who was close to me and whom I cherished, and who travelled a very great distance at the beginning of the war to return here, only to hang herself unbeknownst to anybody in some god-forsaken back-of-the-beyond.

Life around me has often been revolutionizingly, indignantly gloomy and unfair, and that has made me a kind of avenger or a defender, militantly zealous and sharp, of its honor, and this has brought me a name and made me happy, although in fact I only suffered for that name and that happiness, I paid for them.

Rilke died in the same way several months after I exchanged letters with him, and so it was too I lost my Georgian friends.[3] . . .

I am guilty before everyone. But what can I do? So here is the novel – it is a part of this debt, proof that at least I *tried*. . . .

The intimacy of your understanding is startling, your comprehension is immediate, on the mark, confidently in charge; only Marina Tsvetaeva could understand in this way, and on the rare occasion, with those breaches of reality and meaning peculiar to him, Mayakovsky – although it is surprising that I even named him. . . .

BETWEEN BORIS PASTERNAK AND ARIADNA EFRON[4]

November 28, 1948
Dear Boris!

. . .

First of all I will tell you about the things that bother me, or that I can't understand completely, or that I do not fully agree with. First of all, the congestion is terrible. To squeeze into 150 pages of typescript so many fates, epochs, cities, years, events, passions, and take away their much needed "cubic space," their space and spaciousness, the air that they need! And it is not by chance, it did not write itself this way (the way "it" sometimes writes itself!). This is a deliberate artistic cruelty, first, to you yourself, for none of our contemporaries that I know of are masters, as you are, of these very spaces, precisely this feeling of the stretch of time. Second, this is cruelty to your characters who literally bump heads in this cramped space. You treat them like criminals by piling them up on double plank beds. . . .

Why is this so? Is it the urge to say the most important thing about the most important thing ("the living word about what is alive," like the title of one of my mother's pieces), so that nothing would seem superfluous, or so that it would seem easy to talk about complex things? But it is just this "simplicity" that complicates everything so that one has to go through your entire journey *à rebours* [in reverse] restoring what you have cast away.

What you have made is a concentrate of fates, epochs, passions, to which the reader – here I'm speaking only for myself – is forced to add the liquid that you have wrung out, to complicate that which you have "simplified." It turns out that all these people – Lara, and Yury, and Tonya, and Pavel, every single one of them lives on a different planet where time works according to different laws, and our 365 days are equal to one of theirs. As a result they simply do not have time for empty conversations, they do not enjoy those carefree, easy days, which the French call *détente*, and they do not speak about trifles nor do they joke – as we do on earth. And there are none of the amusing moments that youth thrives on. I have no sense of their gradual development or their capacity for development. . . .

About Lara: she is more than just a writer's success, she is more than probable, she just *is*, right now, she's alive right now. And therefore when I write you about her, I am not writing as one would about a heroine, but about a living person whose fate depends on you alone. Let her have all 365 days in the year, and not only the days when some great event and experience happens! Let her get herself to the point of shooting at Komarovsky and do not replace that process with several pages of deliberately dry patter, for example: "life became loathsome to Lara," or: "she started to go mad," or: "she was tempted to reject everything that was close to her," or: "with the intention of shooting at V[iktor] I[ppolitovich Komarovsky], if he should refuse her, misunderstand her or in some other way humiliate her." After all, the action itself is not so important, perhaps, as what leads up to it and makes it inevitable. In this instance the shot is not inevitable, and not because one could manage without it (that is impossible, Lara could not do otherwise!), but because at the most crucial time, at the height of the action, you replaced Lara, you spoke for her in your own (and this time not really even in your own) words, you summed up in a few phrases several extremely agonizing, crucial years, the whole incubation period during which she bore in herself this shot, which had not yet even reached her consciousness, much less rung out. . . .

Forgive me for this faultfinding, dear Boris. It is, perhaps, terribly petty, but the fact is that I bow down to your all-powerful god of detail. I so love in you, in your work, this combination of detail and breadth, that spaciousness of yours in which the knots of human fates are interlaced, untwisted, and cut that I simply get angry when you start to tame and harden yourself, and when you become suddenly stingy in a way that is alien to you.

Oh, what space this book demands, how it cries out for it, and how you can and must expand all this so that there will be air and not bags of oxygen. Do not tell me that you know what you are doing and that you are doing what you know; believe me when I say that I too (without being boastful and importunate) know well enough what you are doing and what you want and must do, and what you must want. I hope this does not sound insolent, but honestly that is the way it is! And I am taking all this so personally and get angry because I fell in love with this book from the first lines to the last and I only want it to fare better.

With the exception of the "crowdedness" mainly between scenes and now and then within them your book is very clean, clear, and simple. And this is its tremendous strength, its advantage over much that you have written. I am speaking, by the way, of clarity and simplicity not only in the sense of "intelligibility," but of that special *limpidité*, which is generally characteristic of your work and which reaches perfection here. The language of all the heroes is superb. Moreover, for all the large numbers of characters in the book, there are no unnecessary people. . . .

As always, your ability to define the undefinable is almost frightening – taste, color, smell, and the sensations, moods, and memories called forth by them, and it is at times like these that we would stake our lives that a word for that does not exist, that is has not been found yet or it is already lost. . . .

The images of Lara, Yura, Pavel, strike us painfully because we knew them just as you drew them, and we loved them, and we lost them because they died, or left, or passed away the way illness, youth, and life pass. The way we ourselves die, leave, or pass away.

As a girl I used to ask myself: where does the past go? How could it be that it was but isn't here now and won't be back again, but it was, it was after all, there was another little girl like me, who sat on this very earth and questioned this very sky: and where is what was? where is that other girl who was just the same and who sought yesterday in just the same way? And so back to the creation of the world.

The very same earth and sky connect us with them [people who lived in the past], and will connect us with the future when we become the past.

How good it is that you have done what only you could do. You didn't let them all slip away nameless and unidentified, you collected them all in your own good and intelligent hands and you brought them to life with your breath and your labor.

You have become stronger and stricter, clearer and wiser.

Thank you.

Do not be angry with my faultfinding, understand my wish for greater space, greater will for those whom I recognized, whom I remembered and came to love thanks to you. . . .

Your Alya

BETWEEN BORIS PASTERNAK AND VARLAM SHALAMOV[5]

[January 1954]
Dear Boris Leonidovich,

I do not know how I should write. This is a letter to you, and a diary, and observations on *Doctor Zhivago* – all together.

I read your novel all the way through. I never thought, and could not imagine to myself even in the my most distant hopes of the last fifteen years, that I would read your unpublished, unfinished novel, and what is more in a manuscript which I received from you yourself. . . .

Your novel raises a great many questions, too many to enumerate and develop in one letter. The first question is about the nature of Russian literature. People learn from writers how to live. They show us what is good, what is bad, they frighten us, they do not allow our soul to bog down in the dark corners of life. Moral pithiness is the distinctive feature of Russian literature. This is feasible only when the truth of human actions, that is, the truth of the characters themselves makes itself felt in the novel. This is different from the truth of observation. It has been a very long time since I read a work of Russian literature that lives up to Tolstoy, Chekhov, and Dostoevsky.

There is no doubt that *Doctor Zhivago* is of this caliber.

And do you know what? I can follow the organization, the composition of the novel, and focus my attention only on that when the author seems to lack the strength to captivate me with his own experiences, thoughts, images, vocabulary. When I want to argue with the author, with his characters, when I can pit my own thoughts against theirs – and either follow them, vanquished or in agreement, or add to them – I speak with his characters as with real people who are in the same room with me – who cares at that point about the architecture of the novel? It probably does exist, like those "internal codes" in *Anna Karenina*, but here I encounter the writer, like a poor reader face to face with his thoughts and feelings – without the novel and its aesthetic fabric.

That is why I don't care whether *D. Zh.* is a novel or sketches of half a century of social custom, or something else again. There are so many thoughts expressed by Vedenyapin, Lara, Zhivago himself that I want to think about, they live in me apart from the novel along with the emotional anxiety that they inspire.

Did you notice (of course you did, after all you see and know everything) that in hundreds and thousands of works there are no *thinking heroes*? It seems to me that this is because there are no *thinking authors*. And even this is being too kind.

I am going to return many times to the thoughts of Vedenyapin, Lara, Zhivago, write them down, recall them at night. . . .

The sobbing boy on the fresh grave, stretching out his hands into the narrative, is splendid.

Now we have grown unused to this kind of weighty prose that demands our attention. – I mean not just the boy, but the novel as a whole.

You never hear people paying respect to the things that for thousands of years troubled the human spirit, that answered its innermost thoughts. It is possible that the best minds and the most ingenious artists have crafted a language for communing with our own best inner self – like all those apostles and later a writer like John Chrysostum who was able to project all the mysteries of the human soul for a thousand years to come. I once read the texts of the liturgy, the texts of the Easter service and the divine services of Holy Week, and I was astonished at their strength, depth, artistry – by the great simplicity of this algebra of the soul. At its root was the Gospel. Tolstoy understood well the all-finiteness [*vsekonechnost'*] of Christ and strove with his frightful strength to raise from the very ground gigantic new trees of life. And what about Luther?

And how can any literate person ignore the questions posed by Christianity?

And how can anyone write a novel about the past without defining a personal attitude toward Christ? That person would surely be put to shame by a simple peasant woman on her way to an all-night vigil, whom he does not see, does not want to see, and he forces himself to think that Christianity does not exist.

And what am I to think after seeing a service in the snow, without any robes, among thousand-year-old larches, with the east for an altar and black squirrels looking on fearfully at the divine service in the taiga. . . .

So what is this novel, and, moreover, who is Doctor Zhivago, who at least until the middle of the novel does not really exist and is still not apparent when Lara Guichard, the genuine heroine of the first half of these pictures – has already reached her full stature in all her charm, a charm only partly borrowed from Turgenev-Dostoevsky – clear, like crystal, sparkling, like the stones of her wedding necklace. Her portrait is a great success, a portrait of such purity that could not be slandered or soiled by the filth of the Komarovskys of the world. I used to know such Laras, well not the same, a little less, a little smaller. She is alive in the novel. She knows something more elevated than all the other characters in the novel, including Zhivago, something more real and important than she could share with someone, much as she might want to.

The name you gave her is very good – Lara is the best Russian name for a woman. It is the name of women who suffered a sorrowful Russian fate – the name of the bride without a dowry, the heroine of a remarkable play, extraordinary for Ostrovsky,[6] and it is also the name of a woman, the heroine of my youth, a woman whom I loved to distraction like a boy, with a love that cleansed and lifted me. . . .

But I do not want to talk about her, but about Larisa Guichard. Absolutely everything is upright in her. Even the very difficult scene of Lara's fall does not call up anything except tenderness and purity. . . . And even when she recalls something loathsome, she "walks as if on air, a proud, animating force." . . .

Your women come off better for you than your men – it seems this is inherent in our greatest writers.

Now let's turn to a question which has been torturing me, which is so out of keeping with the book, which, together with the most important thoughts, observations of nature miraculous is their precision, closely linked to the moods of the heroes, with the unity of the "moral and physical world," with the brightest image of what has been achieved and realized in the novel, represents a crude, glaring phenomenon which ill suits the whole structure of the novel and which makes me ache for you as an artist.

I am talking about the language of the simple people in your novel.

Only about the language and not the psychological justification of these people's actions. The language of the people as you have it – it is all the same no matter whether it be a worker, a peasant, or a domestic servant who is speaking. Besides that, you make it identical for all these groups, which is impossible even now, but all the more so in earlier times, with the greater differences that existed between these segments of the population. Your language of the people is that of a newsrag, and nothing more. I know this language all too well. Their vocabulary is poor, and the poverty of the vocabulary is compensated mainly by intonations sprinkled with swear words; without those this language lacks any kind of character. In peasant life there are more aphorisms, usually the widely known ones; the language of the domestic servant is barren, but generally clean, workers also speak an ordinary language and do not even like verbal embroidery or any artistic coloring.

Maybe the best spot in the book is the part about Rome and Christ – the diary of [Uncle Nikolai] Vedenyapin. I recopied this wonderful part for myself and perhaps I shall learn it by heart. . . .

The Jewish question in which everything is so complicated is stated forcefully – and each person will have to confront this question consciously and clearly. . . .

Your words about the second revolution which is so personal for each of us are very good, as is this whole piece in general. And only Larisa, with her imponderable look, Larisa, inwardly richer than Doctor Zhivago and much more so than Pasha – Larisa is a magnet for everyone, including Zhivago.

I have read 200 pages of the novel – where is Doctor Zhivago? This is a novel about Larisa. . . .

Strelnikov is very good with his natural gift that forces him to call dirty clothes "clean," and crumpled clothes "ironed." The author shows very importantly, and Strelnikov emphasizes, so that the reader may not forget, that Galliulin, a commander of White units, has a more proletarian background than Strelnikov, a commander of Red units. The arguments about the unscrupulousness of the heart, about the gift of accepting the unexpected [*dar nechaiannosti*] are interesting and true.

It seems to me a higher principle of moral philosophy – this very unscrupulousness of the heart.

I was nodding in agreement with everything and just now caught myself: am I not deceiving myself, was it the *novel* that induced me to think that I had felt all these things before, although this sensation just now seemed to have been brought on by another person's words. No. These sensations are close to mine, maybe mine are not as full, not as clearly and completely expressed.

Russia is spring flood, the elements, but not the freedom of animal drives. It is the phenomenon of the best *human* qualities in humanity to whom the chance to mature and excel has been given.

The major characters are alive: Lara, Zhivago, Tonya. Among the minor characters: Komarovsky. But Vedenyapin, however important he may be for the novel, is much paler, as is Gromeko.

The novel is not complete. Why Evgraf?

The way the spectre of death aids in the recovery of one's health? . . .

I do not know how official critics will like the novel. The reader who has not yet been weaned from genuine literature is waiting for just this sort of novel. And for me, an ordinary reader who has long yearned for genuine books, this novel will remain a great event for a long, long time. Here questions which no self-respecting person can ignore are posed with force. Here living heroes of our tragic time, which is after all also my time, have emerged in their full lyric charm. Here the remarkable eye of the artist saw so much that is new in nature, and his brush used the most delicate colors in order to bring out the spiritual condition of humanity.

Here is sketched the "world on the road" that Gogol foresaw, the

Russian spring flood of the civil war [1918–21], of "Russia in wagons," the world moved off of its thousand-year-old moorings, floating off somewhere. I will return again to praise spring, spring floods. . . .

I can't touch on everything in such a short note. I would like to write about Blok, Jewishness, a question in which nothing is simple, but nevertheless a question for each and every person – one of the major, fundamental questions. The family in which I grew up in the Russian province; my father taking me as a young boy to the synagogue, saying: "look – there is the temple where people found God before we did. The truth is the desire for the truth." Something of that sort.

This is an attempt to return Russian literature to its genuine themes and its general ideas. This is an attempt to answer those questions which thousands of people raised both here and abroad, answers to which they have awaited anxiously and in vain in the thousands of novels of the last decades, not believing the newspaper and not understanding poetry.

Two more of this kind of novel and Russian literature is saved. . . .

What makes the novel really remarkable and unique in all of Russian literature is that same quality that animates both *The Childhood of Louvers* and your incomparable poetry; it is to be found in the unusual subtlety with which you depict nature, and what is more, the union of the moral and physical world, your singular skill in linking the one with the other into one whole, and more than linking them together but fusing them so that nature lives together in harmony with the characters' emotional reversals. This device is often used for contrast, for juxtaposition. Sometimes it works. The subtlety here is essential because, after all, the subtle shades of nature, as you show them, are not sufficient in themselves, put into some more or less suitable context. The characters' lives go on, the plot of the novel develops side by side with nature, and nature itself is part of the plot. I am not using the correct terminology, but you will understand what I mean. . . .

Turkmen[istan], January 8, 1956
Dear Boris Leonidovich,

Thank you for the wonderful New Year's gift. For me there is nothing on earth more pleasant, touching, or needed. I feel that I can still live while you are living, while you are alive – excuse me for this bit of sentimentality.

And now to business. What is best in the second book of *D. Zh.* is unquestionably its judgments, appraisals, estimations – clear, written with the clarity of a sketch: one wants to copy, learn, remember them. These are mainly the judgments of Yury Zhivago himself, but the doctor is not the only one to borrow the author's voice. In bad novels there is always one "select" mouthpiece. But here all the heroes use the author's voice – people and forest, and stone, and sky. And one needs to listen to everyone: Sima, and Larisa, and Tyagunova, and Tanya, the laundry girl, and the others. In this – in its new, unusually true judgments – lies the main strength of the novel. In its judgments about a time that is waiting impatiently for someone to say an honest word about it. Whole chapters: "Varykino," "Opposite the House of Sculptures," "The Rowan Tree," Larisa at the coffin – the judgments about art, inspiration, the doctrine of the immaculate conception, Marxism, the evaluation of time are all very, very good – all of them are true – that is, they are intelligible and close to me. Yes, and everyone who reads the novel, as far as I can tell, is very moved by this quality, all of your readers in their own ways. All your judgments of the historical period are correct, although they are given glancing back, from a future that has now become the present. But in this very way they become still more convincing. Everything that Zhivago was able to say – everything is real, meaningful, and alive, and this is a lot, and yet little compared to what he could have said.

There is a tremendous number of valuable observations in the novel, fires unexpectedly blazing up, like the pillar which Zhivago does not notice as he was leaving, or the nightingale, the invisible captivity, or the doctor's pamphlets read by the master of an apartment in front of the woodcutter [Zhivago] or the amulet with the

same prayer worn by both the Partisan and the White Guard soldiers. And much, much more. The poems in the appendix are woven
well into the whole fabric of the novel. I was fascinated by the way
they were interpolated into the novel.

The second indisputable merit of the novel is those extraordinary
landscape watercolors which, as in the first part, stand at the heights
of greatness. In general, and in more than just the landscapes, the
second book concedes nothing to the first, and even surpasses it. The
rowan-tree is splendid, the snow, the sunsets, the forest, and just
everything. The rainy day in two colors, the manuscript of birch, the
leaves in the sun's rays that hide a person – everything, everything.

The landscape in Tolstoy is indifferent to the hero, its description
is self-contained: the burdock in "Hadji Murat" and the grass in the
prison courtyard of *Resurrection* – these are symbols or epigraphs of a
certain kind, but not the fabric of the thing itself.

Dostoevsky has no landscape (which of course, in an indirect way,
gives supports to your definition of art as an independent impulse
which enters any situation and forces everything surrounding to
serve it. Remember Tsvetaeva's article on poetry as a single Poet.
This formula also touches tangentially on this issue).

In his landscapes Chekhov juxtaposes the external and internal
world ("An Attack of Nerves," "The Steppe"). Your landscape is
more external, underscoring the internal world of the hero – an
emotional understanding of this internal world.

About the characters. Doctor Zhivago finally takes his true place
among the major characters. He is an intelligent and good person
who attracts everyone to himself; everyone loves him, or at least each
person retrieves in him a personal, real humanity that had been lost
in life's bustle, in life's battles. By helping him and lightening his life
and everyday worries, everyone pays a debt, a kind of fine for not
keeping what was bestowed in childhood or what life took away.
Thus it is with Samdevyatov and Strelnikov, and Liberius, and naturally the women, with their pragmatic attitude and their tendency to
sacrifice. Even his third wife, Marina, who truly loves him and never
abuses his image, is important. All these different kinds of love,

Tonya's, Larisa's, and Marina's – all of which nevertheless form a united whole – come through very well. There is a sense of doom about Larisa, a sense of unhappiness, of a failed life. This person who illuminates everything good in the novel falls under under life's wheels, crushed, trampled. Everything that I wrote to you about her before is not one bit less true in the second half, but it is just that fate is bitter. But that's the way it needs to be.

I found nothing false in the lives of the main characters. True, after the first part I imagined that the novel would turn out differently, but this way is good, too. I thought that here is an intellectual who is thrown into the whirlpool of life in revolutionary Russia with its Asiatic accents, a whirlpool which, as time is showing, is terrible not because it is a dangerous spring flood, but because of that depraved evil which the whirlpool leaves behind for whole decades; Doctor Zhivago will be slowly and naturally crushed, mortified somewhere in penal servitude. As it happened, the nineteenth century was killed in the camps of the twentieth century. Funerals take place somewhere in a stone pit – a naked and bony corpse with a plywood nameplate (all the packing boxes were used for these nameplates) attached to the left ankle in case the body might be exhumed. . . .

Your, V. Shalamov

August 11, 1956
Dear Boris Leonidovich,

Let me tell you again, probably for the thousandth time, if you count all my conversations by myself with you, that I am proud of you, I believe in you, I idolize you.

I know that you hardly need my weak words, I know that you have more than enough emotional steadfastness, lucidity, and strength to choose your own path on these unprecedented heights, your life is really a fairytale for our corrupted time, and that none of the usual temptations or ordinary enticements will deceive you.

I never wrote you this, but it has always seemed to me that you are the conscience of our age – what Lev Tolstoy was for his time.

Despite the baseness and cowardice of the world of writers, the disregard for everything that is part of the proud and great calling of a Russian writer, the lowering of moral standards, the spiritual beggarliness of all these people who continue to be called Russian writers by some astonishing and awful whim of fate, who lead young people astray, for whom even the gunshot of a suicide cannot punch a hole in this deaf wall – despite all of this life continues in the depths and underground streams and will always be as it used to be, with its craving for genuine truth, nostalgic for the truth; life which, despite everything, has a right to genuine art and to genuine writers.

Here I am talking – as you well know – not just about honesty or the decency of a moral person and writer. Here I am talking about something more – about those things without which art cannot survive. And here is the main point: aren't we really confronting the issue of Russia's honor, the issue, after all, of what exactly a Russian writer is? Really, isn't that right? Isn't your responsibility really at this level? You took upon yourself this responsibility with all steadfastness and fortitude. And all the rest is empty, worthless. You are the honor of our time, you are its pride. In the future our time will be justified by the fact that you lived in it.

I bless you. I am proud of the straightness of your road. I am proud that you did not want to step back one bit from the important purpose of your life. The circumstances of the past year gave you yet another opportunity to work for Mammon by betraying yourself just a little. But you did not want to do that.

God bless you. You will win this great battle, beyond any doubt. Yours Always, V. Shalamov

BETWEEN BORIS PASTERNAK AND N. P. SMIRNOV[7]

April 2, 1955 [Peredelkino]
Dear Nikolai Pavlovich!

. . .

I want very much for you to read the novel and the poetry [of *Doctor Zhivago*], and as concerns the latter: copy them or ask someone else to copy them if you need to.

There are three notebooks of prose . . . in the first book of the novel. I am working on the second which is now finished and contains the end of the novel. I am making a fair copy of it by hand with the almost constant changes that a manuscript always undergoes when its author copies it. This second book is probably stylistically paler and less polished (and so it will stay), but fuller in terms of the plot – gloomier, more tragic.

Here is why I am talking to you about this in such detail. You cannot possibly like this prose. I began to write it in those years after the war when, long before the Zoshchenko and Akhmatova incidents, I found myself distracted by my own feelings of alienation, and I began to stray further and further from the beaten track. I lost my artistic focus, inwardly let myself go, like a weakened bow-string – I wrote this prose unprofessionally, without a consciously sustained creative goal, in the worst sense tamely, with a dullness and naïveté which I permitted myself and forgave. It is very uneven, unraveled, no one likes it much, there are a monstrous multitude of unnecessary characters in it (a part of them, it is true, do return in the second book), then in the course of the exposition they disappear.

But I could not do otherwise. It would be even worse, given my natural feelings of alienation from literary life and having no real intention of ever returning to it, and working only at translation, if I had continued on as before, faithful to style and in the passion of mastery, "to serve the muses," to write as if for publication, and so forth.

This would be a pose, I would be fooling myself, it would be something unreal and false. There are two words, and two concepts related to them, that I do not love (or else I have misunderstood): "wisdom" and "romanticism." It seems to me that these are things without which one can do quite well, things which neither exist nor occur in life, two forms which require neither liberty nor unjustifiable tolerance.[8] So writing in the same way, whether for publication or not, would be romanticism uncharacteristic of me.

Dear Nikolai Pavlovich, tell me something in this regard when you have read the notebooks. You are such a keen person, and so close to me in your view of the world, and such an expert on all this "music," such a good judge of it.

Your, B. Pasternak

April 28, 1955
Dear Nikolai Pavlovich!

Valeria Dmitrievna[9] told me about two weeks ago that she gave you the manuscript. This is not a reminder to return it. Hold on to it as long as you want. But if you have something to tell me and you wish to write me a few lines, do this in the usual way by writing to my city address.

I am afraid that if you enclose a note in the manuscript when you return it or ask my family too gently to pass something on to me, your piece of paper could lie around somewhere without my knowing it or it could be mislaid. Meanwhile we are accustomed to passing letters along by hand.

Did you receive my letter? Whatever low opinion I may have had about the second book of Zhivago, I am now finishing it, and bringing it to a conclusion is my duty to myself.

But this urge to write modestly, without special effects and stylistic coquetry – which increasingly has been tormenting me – has led me probably too far into the realm of those virtues that are opposed to art; and after I had left a nervous style of writing marked with that energy which is required for an artist, I appropriated an aimless, unexpressive thoroughness that hampers my best intentions.

And from all points you hear: why are you writing prose? Is this your business?

Heartfelt greetings.

Your, B. Pasternak.

BETWEEN BORIS PASTERNAK AND JOHN HARRIS[10]

February 8, 1959
Dear Friend,

I don't believe my eyes to have at last reached the happy moment to answer (or only to venture it) your three last letters, precious, pithy, profound. . . .

Now, being overloaded with troubles, annoyances, correspondence and so on, I must attempt to limit myself to what is the most striking and interesting in your letters, to the question or even to the philosophy of coincidences.

I can do it only in a shortness that opposes itself to the vastness and complexity of the subject. My heavenly English will not be the only reason to make you laugh. My ignorance revealing itself in my "scientific" parallels will also surprise you. But I overleap too hastily an essential point. I come back to your letters.

You were perfectly right on remembering Donne, his sense of living totality, his "he is us." And your Harris theory: "Coincidence is Pasternak's *poetic method* of saying something like Donne . . . etc." is, if not the truth itself, then a guess near by in a distance of only a few steps from it.

There are aphorisms, definitions, statements in my novel. But the chief participation of thought in it does not lie in these open sentences (opinions) uttered in dialogues, author's notes etc. etc.; but in the hidden tendency which penetrates the very manner of my display of reality, of my description. Here, in my change of times, style of movement, character of colours, arrangement of groups is my latent unsaid philosophy. I could say more: my philosophy itself, as a whole, is in general rather an *inclination* than a conviction. And you were right, I repeat, to refer yourself to Donne. What matters in this case are not the different separate notions and sayings, but the constant peculiar light in which everything is seen, lived, reflected, and said.

The last century still conserved the old rationalist meaning of causality as of a unique, firmly forged, iron chain of causes and effects, antecedences and consequences linked together. Such were the laws of logic and mathematics, such the natural laws.

The idea of the strict casual [*sic*] order and of retribution partly influenced the art. For instance, the height, the pick of Flaubert's or Maupassant's narrative beauty consisted in their style, in the fatalism of their inexorable and pitiless sentence-construction, as if their novels were not free descriptions of regularly running law-governed lives but involuntary prescriptions or written verdicts for the very destinies.

I am terribly behind the actual knowledge, I am an ignorant. I am surely quite wrong, but I have a feeling, that the modern science is inclined to present its own first foundations not in the old a-priori shape but in a certain form of so to say statistically . . . obtained principles. It is not induction, but an admission of other, imaginary or even unimaginable cases, rivaling with the regularity and vanquished by its incomparable prevalence – as I conceive it.

I cannot deny causality, of course. But unlike the determinism of the great novelists of the past I will give credence to my leadings, not to persuasions. Thur artistical ambition was in the outlines, contours, limits of the objectivity, in the delineation of its structural frames. And that is the most submitted to the mechanics of fate.

I cannot get rid of the fancy, that the *filling* of those strictly ruled forms, the stuffs, the colours, spirits, moods, all that poetry expresses by comparisons and images, all these *contents* (of life and arts) are of another, a little milder origin, more accessible to choice, independent. The recurrence of poetry to *comparison* in their treatment betrays the relatively free-er nature of these things: their ability of being chosen, modified, replaced. I always aspired from poetry to prose, to the narrative and descriptive dealing with ambient reality, because such prose is the sequel and completion of what is or means poetry for me. In accordance with it I could say: poems are undeveloped, unrealized prose.

Prose is for me the representation of life, reality, surrounding or better the picture and the show of the manner how I see, perceive and interpret it. The objective world in my habitual, natural grasping, is a vast infinite inspiration, that sketches, erases, chooses, compares and describes and composes itself. It is an other, immensely greater "I" than I myself, hardly anyhow peculiarly connected with me (in no different way than with you), but to cognize is to assimilate, and this likening (between the world and the subject) is the principal feature of my perception. Life (not generally, but more exactly: "Life that I will picture") – life, living, moving reality in such rendering must have a touch of spontaneous subjectivity, even of arbitrariness, wavering, tarrying, doubting, joining and disjoining elements, substituting one through another. Over and above the times, events and persons there is a nature, a spirit of their very succession. The frequent coincidences in the plot are (in this case) not the secret trick expedients of the novelist. They are traits to characterize that somewhat willful, free, fanciful flow of reality. Not the author resorts to coincidences as to bad unravelling; by the by, final solutions are not my requirements at all; the novelist, in my understanding, needs them less than the historian – not the author has recourse to coincidences, but he describes the whole, the "halo" of the objectivity as sparing, as economizing itself in coincidences (as it occurs with "ominous" incidents of everyday life to us all) the choice of its possibilities, the waste of its imaginative means.

But perhaps it is exactly the ancient deus ex machina, only turned (in this system) into virtue from vice.

(Febr. 16, 1959) It is folly to send you this stupid incomprehensible letter written in an unknown language. But when will I write you a better one? The hindrances and surprises will not cease, and the new ones surpass the precedent.

[unsigned]

BETWEEN BORIS PASTERNAK AND STEPHEN SPENDER[11]

August 9, 1959

I am honored enormously by your letter giving rise to mutual personal acquaintance.

A rare opportunity presents itself to accelerate and secure my answer. It must be used to-day – no: within an hour.

The question about Mr. Edm. Wilson's explanatory note to *Dr. Zh.*, is for me not of such flat categorical importance as a chain of talks, penslips in letters and inaccurately transmitted reports seems to be susceptible to ascribe them to. I did not see the April Number of *Encounter* where the study was published, I was only spoken about it in letters from America, West Germany, and France. (By the way: the article by Stuart Hampshire was excellent, especially his un-awaited, uncommon, and nevertheless true and sharp insight on Shakespeare's influence.)

Edm. Wilson is a great name to me, a real judge and interesting writer on artistic matters. I was flattered on hearing him to have a notion of me. I have no reason to enter into an argument with him. What is poetry – understanding? Can there be a right one, a false one?

But it should be a great pleasure for me to write a few pages for *Encounter* in the only form I can allow myself (even that one being a very stretched admission). I shall write you a personal letter touching that, alien to me, detailed allegorical interpretation of literature as a point of contiguity to deeper and more essential reflections. It must remain a letter, it is not permitted to become an article manifestly composed by myself. That is to say: an other contributor of your monthly (not you, God forbid. . . . I dare not admit that more trou-ble and pain and burdens should fall upon you by my fault beside your numberless own) – another member of the editorship, if will-ing, must use the essence of the letter *in quotations* (having translated my gibberish in true English) and present the whole as his own compositon with my, contracted from my letters, content or stuffing.

A possibility to have a short article of mine as such, as an article openly written and signed by me and also to be printed, is on hand. It is my short essay on Fr. Chopin, written more than ten years ago in Russian. I have sent a manuscript of it to Mr. Richard Newnham for the Penguin Books. If it should be interesting for you and the Pen-guins would consent, would you not be willing to insert in the paper these two or three columns translated? It was published in Russian (perhaps not in the same arrangement) soon after the war.

My Tricks and devices shall not amaze you:

And this poor clerk with world-offended eyes
Builds with red hands his heaven; makes our bones
The necessary scaffolding to peace . . .

It continues in all its strictness. My situation is worse, more un-bearable and endangered than I can say or you think of.

The letter on art, literature, and so on, I shall write and mail you registered by post after having had your reply.

Sincerely yours,

B. Pasternak

Excuse the hasty emptiness of the letter.

August 22, 1959

It is, as I said last time, a great pleasure, honour, and thrill for me to write you. But I am aware of the onus that will fall on the person you will choose and entrust with my letter to find out the sense of its gibberish and to transform it in the English shape when using it to literary purpose.

I have no other debts to Mr. Edmund Wilson than to pay him gratitude and admiration. Each critic's right is to comment the im-pression produced on him by a work of art in the manner he likes it or is accustomed to. I am asked to write brief prefaces, introductory accounts, preambling editions, selections, performance of Bloch (for Italy), of Tolstoy and Lermontov (for America), of Chekhov (for India).

I am no explorer, no erudite. I have read very little in my life, and what I have read, I have it for the most part forgotten. I shall write all them short letters on the many topics, conveying only my general subjective idea on the matter, just so as Mr. Wilson does on my behalf.

If I say, for instance, Chekhov's singularity as a playwright and the chief merit and value of his plays consisted in his having inscribed man in a landscape on equal terms with trees and clouds; that as a dramatist he was againt the over-rating of the social and the human; that the conversational texts of the plays are not written in obedience to any logic of interests, passion, characters, or plots, but that the cues and speeches are taken and snatched out of the space and the air they were spoken, like spots and strokes of a forest or a meadow only to render the true simultaneous resemblance by the subject of the play;

to life in the far broader sense of a unique vast inhabited frame, to its symmetries and dissymmetries, proportions and disproportions – to life as a hidden mysterious principle on the whole.

If Chekhov should live and have read these words, would he ever consent? Why should Mr. Wilson's liberty and licenses be less than mine?

Only I don't esteem accessories and details of such an importance. Rather their comparative *indifference* has a special deliberate meaning, being one of the means of my language, the real tongue of my thought.

When we take the great novel of the last century in its essence, extolled and idolised, for instance, by Henry James. When we examine the greatest, Dostoevsky, Tolstoy, Dickens, Flaubert. When from the fabric of a *Madame Bovary*, we gradually, one after another, subtract characters, their development, situations, occurrences, the plot, the subject, the content. . . . The second-rate diverting literature will leave no remainder after such a subtraction. But the name creation (or, for example, *David Copperfield*) lets remain the *cardinal*: the characterisation of reality as such; almost as of a philosophic category; as a member or link of our minds universe; as life's perpetual companion and surroundings.

For this characterisation of reality of the being, as a substratum, as a common background, the nineteenth century applied the incontestable doctrine of causality, the belief that the objectivity was determined and ruled by an iron chain of causes and effects, that all appearances of the moral and material world were subordinate to the law of sequels and retributions. And the severer and more inflexible was an author in showing such consequences (of characters and conducts) the greater a realist he was esteemed. The tragic bewitching spell of Flaubert's style or Maupassant's manner roots in the fact that their narratives are irrevocable like verdicts or sentences, beyond recall.

I also from my earliest years have been struck by the observation that existence was more original, extraordinary, and inexplicable than any of its separate astonishing incidents and facts. I was attracted by the unusualness of the usual. Composing music, prose, or poetry I was driven by definite conceptions and motifs, I pursued certain favourite objects and themes. But the top pleasure consists in having hit the sense or taste of reality, in having been able, in having succeeded in rendering the *atmosphere of being*, the surrounding whole, the total environment, the frame, where the particular and depicted thing is having been plunged and floating.

But curiously enough, while pondering over the distinctive notes or features of *life perception* (of recognised *existence*) for the purpose of evoking the same sensations through art's expressive attempts I come to results if not diametrically opposite to the tendencies of the named masterpieces, so at least to quite different observations than those of our predecessors and teachers.

If I had to represent a broad, a large picture of living reality, I would not hope to heighten its sense of *extant objectivity* by accentuating the fixed statics of anakē; of natural laws, of settled moral regularity.

To attain a true resemblance between the imitative efforts of art and the truly tasted and experienced order of life it would me not suffice to put my representation in a vivid instantaneous motion. I would pretend (metaphorically) to have seen nature and universe themselves not as a picture made or fastened on an immovable wall, but as a sort of painted canvas roof or curtain in the air, incessantly pulled and blown and flapped by a something of an immaterial unknown and unknowable wind.

Whether it was the scarce and sparse knowledge of the different physical waves as external impellents to our subjective sensual date; or as an aftertaste of the legend of world creation; whether it was a kind of feeling derived from the notion of life's being placed in the narrow space between birth and death, but always my sense of the whole, of the reality as such was that of a reached sending, of a sudden unawaited coming, of a welcomed arrival and I always sought to reproduce this trait of being sent and launched, that I thought to find in the nature of the appearance.

That is the only thing I could not oppose, but add to any allegorically directed detailed criticism: that behind and above all stressed and pointed trifles (even on their sharpened magic) and besides the importance of described human lots and historical events there is an effort in the novel to represent the whole sequence of facts and beings and happenings like some moving entireness, like a developing, passing by, rolling and rushing inspiration, as if reality itself had freedom and choice and was composing itself out of numberless variants and versions.

Hence the not sufficient tracing of characters I was reproached with (more than to delineate them I tried to efface them); hence the frank arbitrariness of the "coincidences" (through this means I wanted to show the liberty of being, its verisimilitude touching, adjoining improbability).

It is too bold and silly to send you this incorrect pell mell unread, unrevised. Only the hurry, wherewith I do it does it justify.

Yours, etc.

Sept[ember] 9, 1959

Best thanks for your lively, exciting letter.

It would be a straw splitting to correct the report you were misguided with of my coming to the front and reciting poems to the soldiers. I don't like declaration. Even in a peaceful society, between comfortable, tranquil folks, I consider such performances as pretentious, contrary on common patience and attention. How many more should I think a blasphemy to have paraded before such an earnest people risking hourly their lives with any kind of literary trifles. Your information is combined out of different parts, each true when taken separately and false when joint together. I went to the front, and I was persuaded or induced to appear publicly during the next postwar years in the concert halls of the rear; and by those recitals I have been surprised to be prompted on every line I forgot or pronounced with a pause or delay. That are mere nonsense. Why am I wasting time on such nothings? Here is why I am touching upon it. Journalism, newspapers, chronicles of events are meant and calculated to be statements of facts, records, evidences, certainties. Is it not curious that this region of supposed realism and practical views, publicity, is the most unreal domain of the melodramatic romanticism, not to speak of its sad tasks that, for observers of this kind, life is a cardboard-opera situation?

Please do me the friendly favour. After having read the short notice on Chopin, estimate quite soberly: (1) is it clear enough (in its original and translated essence) as to make its pith to be understood (the particular nature of the now formal, now wanted by the contemporary taste, new, original, rich of detailed content and meaning, lived, experienced through and through, personally endured, documentary art). (2) will it not look odd in print, its (of the article) simplicity and shortness or leading to misunderstandings as if arguing against anyone or anything?

To one of my nearest friends in Germany . . . I wrote a month ago much about music, form, content, realism, romanticism. She replied (we are great friends) she could not retain the essence of the letter only for herself and would try to have published some excerpts in the Hamburger paper *Die Welt* I doubt, I don't believe in the possibility of such extracts out of the tousy, styleless, negligent letter. But if she has got it done and published, perhaps the passages can serve you as additions or as footnotes to the Chopin matter if it is needed? (The correspondence goes in German.)

This letter is only a cover or a wrapping to my thanks to you.

Yours sincerely,

NOTES

Translations are by Charlotte Hoss and Edith W. Clowes.

1. Olga Mikhailovna Freidenberg (1890–1955) was a cousin of Pasternak who lived in Leningrad. She was a literary critic and a classicist. The letters included here first appeared in Boris Pasternak, *Perepiska s Ol'goi Freidenberg*, ed. Elliott Mossman (New York: Harcourt, Brace, Jovanovich, 1981).

2. This is a veiled reference to the Akhmatova and Zoshchenko affairs earlier in 1946 during which the shortlived postwar "thaw" in literary politics came to an abrupt end.

3. Pasternak exchanged letters with the Czech-born Austrian poet Rainer Maria Rilke in April–May 1926. Rilke passed away on December 29, 1926. Paolo Yashvili and Titsian Tabidze perished in 1937; one committed suicide, the other was arrested.

4. Ariadna Sergeevna Efron (1913–75), the daughter of Marina Tsvetaeva, was arrested in 1939 and sentenced to eight years in prison. The letter about *Doctor Zhivago* was written by her in Riazan where, after having served her full camp term, she for a short time was allowed to live and work. In February 1949 she was again arrested. The letter included here first appeared in Ariadna Efron, *Pis'ma iz ssylki* (Paris: YMCA Press, 1982).

5. Varlam Tikhonovich Shalamov (1907–82), son of a priest, served time in Kolyma. He wrote stories and sketches about his experiences in prison camp, the most famous of which are collected in the volume *Tales of Kolyma*. The letters reproduced here first appeared in *Iunost'* 10 (1988): 54–67.

6. *The Dowerless Bride* [*Bednaia nevesta*], written in 1850–51 by Aleksandr Ostrovsky.

7. A literary critic living in Leningrad. These letters first appeared in "'Vtorzhenie voli v sud'bu': pis'ma B. L. Pasternaka v sviazi s "Doktorom Zhivago","" ed. Elena V. Pasternak, *Russkaia rech'* 1 (1990): 3–16.

8. And "wisdom" is a type of false depth, and often even a kind of mental opaqueness for which the key has not yet been found (Pasternak's note).

9. The wife of writer Mikhail Prishvin.

10. An English schoolteacher. These letters, written in English, were first published in *Scottish Slavonic Review*, (1984): 82–94.

11. An English poet and critic. These letters, written in English, first appeared in *Encounter* 83 (August 1960): 3–6.

IV   SELECT BIBLIOGRAPHY

Emphasis is placed on publications since 1985. See the Sendich and Greber bibliography for the fullest available list of publications before 1985, and Cornwell, *Pasternak's Novel*, for a discussion of critical trends before 1985.

Aucouturier, Michel. "The Metonymous Hero or the Beginnings of Pasternak the Novelist." In *Pasternak: A Collection of Critical Essays*, edited by V. Erlich, 43–50. Englewood Cliffs, N.J.: Prentice-Hall, 1978.

Bakhnov, L. V., and L. B. Voronin, eds. *S raznykh tochek zreniia: "Doktor Zhivago" Borisa Pasternaka*. Moscow: Sovetskii pisatel', 1990.

    A "white book" on the Pasternak affair. Contains the referee report on *Doctor Zhivago* of the editors of *Novyi mir* from 1956, a number of the responses in the Soviet press following the announcement of the Nobel Prize in 1958, personal correspondence, and some recent Russian reviews of *Doctor Zhivago* since 1988.

Barnes, Christopher. *Boris Pasternak: A Literary Biography*. Vol. 1, *1890–1928*. Cambridge: Cambridge University Press, 1990.

    The most thorough English-language biography of Pasternak to date. Warns against seeing early work only as preparation for *Doctor Zhivago*.

———. "Pasternak, Dickens and the Novel Tradition." *Forum for Modern Language Studies* 26, no. 4 (October 1990): 326–41.

    Comparison to Dickens's *A Tale of Two Cities* helps to explain such difficult aspects of *Doctor Zhivago* as the use of coincidences to build the plot and of "deus ex machina" characters.

Bethea, David. "*Doctor Zhivago*: The Revolution and the Red Crosse Knight." In *The Shape of Apocalypse in Modern Russian Fiction*, 230–68. Princeton: Princeton University Press, 1989.

    Discusses Pasternak's attempt to bridge the gap between the material and the mystical in his concept of history. Draws on the thought of Husserl, Bergson, and Fyodorov.

Birnbaum, Henrik. "Further Reflections on the Poetics of *Doktor Zhivago*: Structure, Technique, and Symbolism." In *Boris Pasternak and His Times*, 284–314. Berkeley and Los Angeles: Berkeley Slavic Specialties, 1989.

    Discusses four issues central to *Doctor Zhivago*: the relationship between the narrative and the poetry cycle, the question of genre, the function of metonymy and metaphor, and the nature of the "simplicity" of Pasternak's style.

Bodin, Per Arne. *Nine Poems from Doktor Živago: A Study of Christian Motifs in Boris Pasternak's Poetry*. Stockholm: Almqvist and Wiksell, 1976.

A systematic analysis of "Hamlet," "Holy Week," "Fairy Tale," "Christmas Star," "Miracle," "Evil Days," "Magdalene I," "Magdalene II," and "The Garden of Gethsemane."

————. "Pasternak and Christian Art." In *Boris Pasternak: Essays*, edited by N. A. Nilsson, 203–14. Stockholm: Almqvist and Wiksell, 1976.

Shows sources for Christian motifs in the Zhivago poems in paintings of Rembrandt, and Breughel, icon painting, and Orthodox liturgy, as well as the New Testament.

Bolt, Robert. *Doctor Zhivago: The Screenplay*. New York: Random House, 1965.

Borisov, Vadim, and Evgenii Pasternak. "The History of Boris Pasternak's Novel 'Doctor Zhivago.'" *Soviet Literature* 2 (1989): 137–50.

An abridged translation of Borisov and Pasternak, "Materialy k tvorcheskoi istorii romana B. Pasternaka 'Doktor Zhivago'" [Materials for a creative history of B. Pasternak's novel, *Doctor Zhivago*], *Novyi mir* 6 (1988): 205–48. Gives quite a thorough discussion of the process of writing *Doctor Zhivago* and Pasternak's intentions.

————. "Materialy k tvorcheskoi istorii romana B. Pasternaka 'Doktor Zhivago'" [Materials for a creative history of B. Pasternak's novel *Doctor Zhivago*]. *Novyi mir* 6 (1988) 205–48.

Clowes, Edith W. "From Beyond the Abyss: Nietzschean Myth in Zamiatin's *We* and Pasternak's *Doctor Zhivago*." In *Nietzsche and Soviet Culture*, edited by B. G. Rosenthal, 313–37. Cambridge: Cambridge University Press, 1994.

Analyzes Iurii's creative experience in the light of Nietzsche's, Berdiaev's, and Ivanov's myth of the creative self.

Cornwell, Neil. *Pasternak's Novel: Perspectives on "Doctor Zhivago."* Keele: University of Keele, Department of Russian Studies, 1986.

A useful survey of the major opinions and critical approaches to *Doctor Zhivago*. Focuses in part on the question of the interaction among author, narrator, and reader.

————. "Soviet Responses to *Doktor Zhivago*." In *From Pushkin to Palisandriia: Essays on the Russian Novel in Honor of Richard Freeborn*, edited by A. McMillan, 201–15. New York: St. Martin's, 1990.

Deals with the Russian critical reception of *Doctor Zhivago* since its first Soviet publication in 1988.

Danow, David K. "Dialogic Poetics: *Doktor Zhivago.*" *Slavic Review* 50, no. 4 (Winter, 1991): 954–64.

While noting the seeming predominance of monologic narrative technique in *Doctor Zhivago*, Danow argues for an overriding dialogic structure in the various "echoes" of Vedeniapin's philosophy in Lara's, Iurii's, Misha's, and Sima's discourse.

———. "Epiphany in 'Doctor Zhivago.'" *Modern Language Review* 76, no. 4 (1981): 889–903.

Notes the lack of psychological motivation in *Doctor Zhivago*, and discusses the major role of perception and language in achieving the moments of revelation or higher consciousness and understanding that form the novel's climactic points.

Erlich, Victor, ed. *Pasternak: A Collection of Critical Essays.* Englewood Cliffs, N.J.: Prentice-Hall, 1978.

Contains five of the best early articles on *Doctor Zhivago*. In "Boris Pasternak," Fyodor Stepun focuses on the novel's links to the symbolist culture of the turn of the century. Gives a sympathetic assessment of key problems in the novel: plot construction, characterization, Pasternak's concept of "personality," political views, philosophy of history. Stuart Hampshire in "*Doctor Zhivago*: As from a Lost Culture" gives a comparatist's evaluation of *Doctor Zhivago*, characterizing it as "naive" literature. In "A Testimony and a Challenge – Pasternak's *Doctor Zhivago*," Victor Erlich argues with the claim that the novel is written in a realist style. Robert Louis Jackson, in "*Doctor Zhivago*: Liebestod of the Russian Intelligentsia," examines the novel as a creative response to Tolstoy's *War and Peace* and finds it closer in spirit to the epic poem "Retribution" of the symbolist poet Aleksandr Blok. Dimitri Obolensky, in "The Poems of *Doctor Zhivago*," gives one of the first analyses of the links between the poems in chapter 17 and the prose narrative that comprises the first sixteen chapters.

Fleishman, Lazar. *Boris Pasternak: The Poet and His Politics.* Cambridge: Harvard University Press, 1990.

A thorough treatment of Pasternak's social, philosophical, and political positions. Includes material from Fleishman's Russian books, *Pasternak v dvadtsatye gody* [Pasternak in the 1920s] and *Pasternak v tridtsatye gody* [Pasternak in the 1930s].

———. "Ot 'Zapisok Patrika' k 'Doktoru Zhivago.'" *Izvestiia ANSSSR. Seriia literatury i iazyka* 50, no. 2 (1991): 114–23.

A helpful comparison of *Doctor Zhivago* to the prose fragments written in the 1930s and a survey of one of the darkest and most silent periods in Pasternak's career.

Gibian, George. "*Doctor Zhivago*, Russia, and Leonid Pasternak's Rembrandt." In *The Russian Novel from Pushkin to Pasternak*, edited by J. Garrard, 203–24. New Haven: Yale University Press, 1983. Translated into Russian and reprinted in *Voprosy literatury* 9 (1988): 104–27. Deals with father's and son's differing attitudes toward Judaism and Boris Pasternak's confrontation with Russian messianism.

Gifford, Henry. *Pasternak: A Critical Study*. Cambridge: Cambridge University Press, 1977. A good general introduction to Pasternak's works. Includes separate chapters on *Doctor Zhivago* and the Zhivago poems.

———. "Pasternak and European Modernism." *Forum for Modern Language Studies* 26, no. 4 (October 1990): 301–14. Claims that *Doctor Zhivago* is not severed from literary modernism but rather gives a summation of Pasternak's modernist aesthetic.

Gimpelevich-Schwartzman, Zina. *Boris Pasternak: What M is out There?* New York: Legas, 1990. Three of the essays collected here deal with aspects of *Doctor Zhivago*: images of Moscow, neo-Kantian ideas, and major themes in the Zhivago poems.

Gorelov, Pavel. "Razmyshleniia nad romanom" [Thoughts on the novel]. *Voprosy literatury* 9 (1988): 54–81. Maintains that one has to read *Doctor Zhivago* as one would a diary or any other fragmented work.

Griffiths, F. T., and S. J. Rabinowitz. "*Doctor Zhivago* and the Tradition of the National Epic." *Comparative Literature* 1 (1980): 63–79.

Harris, Jane Gary. "Pasternak's Vision of Life: The History of a Feminine Image." *Russian Literature TriQuarterly* 9 (1974): 410–17. Emphasizes the symbolic quality of Pasternak's feminine images.

Ivanova, Natal'ia. "Iskuplenie" [Redemption]. In *S raznykh tochek zreniia*, edited by L. V. Bakhnov et al., 190–211. Moscow: Sovetskii pisatel', 1990. Analyzes the contrapuntal interaction of the themes of life and death in *Doctor Zhivago*.

———. "Smert' i voskresenie doktora Zhivago" [The Death and Resurrection of Doctor Zhivago]. *Iunost'* 5 (1988): 78–82. Excerpt reprinted in *Russkii iazyk za rubezhom* 2 (1990): 104–5.

Josipovici, Gabriel. "A Mistaken Position." *Times Literary Supplement* 4532 (February 9–15, 1990): 135–36.

Gives a negative assessment of *Doctor Zhivago* as a melodrama. Critical of the characters' ethnic views, especially concerning Jews. Calls for greater attention to Pasternak's problematic views on his own Jewish heritage.

Kelly, Ian Crawford. "Eternal Memory: Historical Themes in Pasternak's 'Doctor Zhivago.'" Ph.D. diss., Columbia University, 1986.

Discusses the meaning of history as eternal memory in *Doctor Zhivago* in the context of the thought of Soloviev, Florenskii, Bulgakov, and Berdiaev.

Kondakov, I. V. "Roman 'Doktor Zhivago' v svete traditsii russkoi kul'tury" [The novel, *Doctor Zhivago*, in the light of the Russian cultural tradition]. *Izvestiia Akademii nauk SSSR. Seriia literatury i iazyka* 49, no. 6 (1990): 527–40.

Finds that *Doctor Zhivago* has gained even greater resonance in the late 1980s than it could have had if it had been published in the 1950s. Russian history and culture have supported Pasternak's insights. Argues for interpreting the novel beyond the historical context of its production in order to appreciate fully how Doctor Zhivago *as a work of art* was able to challenge a totalitarian system that denied art.

Lekic, Maria. "Pasternak's *Doktor Živago*: The Novel and its Title." *Russian Language Journal* 141–43 (1988): 177–91.

Reviews various early titles of *Doctor Zhivago* and analyzes the theme of immortality shared by some of them.

Levi, Peter. *Boris Pasternak*. London: Century Hutchinson, 1990.

A popular biography written by a literary journalist. Deals in detail with the Zhivago poems.

Likhachev, Dmitrii S. "Razmyshleniia nad romanom B. L. Pasternaka 'Doktor Zhivago.'" *Novyi mir* 1 (1988): 5–10.

Reprinted in *S raznykh tochek zreniia*. Comments on the genre of *Doctor Zhivago*.

Livingstone, Angela. *Boris Pasternak: Doctor Zhivago*. Cambridge: Cambridge University Press, 1989.

A short introduction to *Doctor Zhivago* with discussion of the novel's reception, biographical background, major characters, historical themes, style, and the poems.

———. "'Integral Errors': Remarks on the Writing of *Doctor Zhivago*." *Essays in Poetics* 13, no. 2 (1988): 83–94.

Argues that mistakes in chronology, tautologies, characters' mistaken perceptions are all a deliberate part of the design of Pasternak's novel.

———. "Pasternak and Faust." *Forum for Modern Language Studies* 26, no. 4 (October, 1990): 353–69.

Reviews Pasternak's encounters with Faust and references to it in *Doctor Zhivago*. Rejects any argument for kinship between Zhivago and Faust.

———, ed. *Pasternak on Art and Creativity*. Cambridge: Cambridge University Press, 1985, 201–62.

Contains selected passages from *Doctor Zhivago* and commentary on aesthetic views expressed there. Outlines a reading of the novel as a "defense of poetry and the poetic vision."

Ljunggren, Anna. "O poeticheskom genezise 'Doktora Zhivago.'" In *Studies in Twentieth-Century Russian Prose*, edited by N. A. Nilsson, 228–49. Stockholm: Almqvist and Wiksell, 1982.

An excellent discussion of characters' and narrator's discourse in the context of the question about the genre of *Doctor Zhivago*. Based on Bakhtin's theory of discourse.

Lönnqvist, Barbara. "From Dewdrops to Poetry: The Presence of Egorij Chrabryj in *Doktor Živago*." *Russian Literature* 34, no. 2 (1993): 161–87.

Unravels the workings of "cultural memory" in *Doctor Zhivago*.

de Mallac, Guy. *Boris Pasternak: His Life and Art*. Norman: University of Oklahoma Press, 1981.

Gives a good intellectual-historical background to *Doctor Zhivago*.

Masing-Delic, Irene. "Capitalist Bread and Socialist Spectacle: The Janus Face of 'Rome' in Pasternak's Doctor Zhivago." In *Boris Pasternak and His Times*, 372–85. Berkeley and Los Angeles: Berkeley Slavic Specialties, 1989.

Gives an allegorical reading in which Komarovskii and Antipov are interpreted in terms of Vedeniapin's theory of Roman history.

———. "Živago's 'Christmas Star' as Homage to Blok." In *Aleksandr Blok: Centennial Conference*, edited by W. N. Vickery, 207–23. Columbus: Slavica, 1984.

Considers the allusions to Aleksandr Blok's poetry in *Doctor Zhivago*.

Maslenikova, Zoia. *Portret Borisa Pasternaka*. Moscow: Sovetskaia Rossiia, 1990.

Reminiscences about conversations with Pasternak in 1958.

Mezhakov-Koriakin, Igor'. "Dvoistvennost' izobrazheniia i vospriiatiia

obraza Iuriia Zhivago v romane Borisa Pasternaka 'Doktor Zhivago'"
[Duplicity of portrayal and reception of the image of Iurii Zhivago in
Boris Pasternak's novel, *Doctor Zhivago*]. *Slavia Orientalis* 37, no. 3
(1988): 443–58.
> Iurii's unattractive social character is compared to that of Maksim
> Gorky's hero, Klim Samgin. By contrast, his mind and philosophy of
> life are admirable.

McInerny, John M. "Lean's *Zhivago*: A Reappraisal." *Literature Film
Quarterly* 15, no. 1 (1987): 43–48.
> Defends the movie's delicate balance between epic and lyric impulses.

Mlikotin, Anthony M. "*Doctor Zhivago* as a Philosophical and Poetical
Novel." *Australian Slavonic and East European Studies* 2, no. 1 (1988):
77–88.
> Argues for harmony of poetic and philosophical elements in *Doctor
> Zhivago*.

Mossman, Elliott. "Metaphors of History in 'War and Peace' and 'Doctor Zhivago.'" In *Literature and History: Theoretical Problems and Russian Case Studies*, edited by Gary Saul Morson, 247–62. Stanford:
Stanford University Press, 1986.
> Contrasts Tolstoy's mechanistic and Pasternak's biological meta-
> phors for history and pursues the assumptions about determinism,
> causality, coincidence, and relativity embedded in these metaphors.

———. "Toward a Poetics of the Novel *Doctor Zhivago*: The Fourth
Typhus." In *Boris Pasternak and His Times*, 386–97. Berkeley: Berkeley Slavic Specialties, 1989.
> Discusses the interaction between death and regeneration in *Doc-
> tor Zhivago* and how it is played out in the novel's complex image
> structures.

Muravina, Nina. *Vstrechi s Pasternakom* [Meetings with Pasternak]. Ten-
afly, New Jersey: Hermitage, 1990.
> These memoirs of a literary critic give insight into the history of
> writing *Doctor Zhivago*. A great deal of interesting information about
> literary culture in the last years of the Stalin regime.

Pasternak, Boris L. *Doctor Zhivago*. Translated by Max Hayward and
Manya Harari. New York: Random House, 1958.
> The standard English translation of *Doctor Zhivago*.

———. *Doctor Zhivago*. Translated by Max Hayward and Manya Harari.
London: Collins Fontana Books, 1958.
> The same basic translation with dozens of minor changes made by
> Mrs. George Villiers and the Marchese Origo.

Pasternak, Evgenii Borisovich. *Boris Pasternak: Materialy dlia biografii* [Boris Pasternak: materials for a biography]. Moscow: Sovetskii pisatel', 1989.

This invaluable compendium of materials on Pasternak's life by his son has been in part published as *Boris Pasternak: The Tragic Years, 1930–1960*, translated by Ann Pasternak Slater and Craig Raine (London: Collins Harvill, 1990). This translation includes parts of only four chapters, leaving out the materials from Pasternak's early life.

———. Letter to the editor. *Voprosy literatury* 12 (1988): 248–54.

Defends Boris Pasternak's views on nationalism and Judaism.

———, ed. "For Boris Pasternak's Birth Centenary." *Soviet Literature* 10 (1990).

Parts of this centenary issue that pertain to *Doctor Zhivago* are "Notes from Various Years," 113–17; E. Pasternak, "Boris Pasternak's Nobel Prize," 128–34; and Lidia Chukovskaia, "From Diary Notes," 135–50.

Payne, Robert. *The Three Worlds of Boris Pasternak*. New York: Coward-McCann, 1961.

Creative biography of Pasternak as poet, novelist, and political figure.

Piskunova, S., and V. Piskunov. "'Vsednevnoe nashe bessmertie'" [Our daily immortality]. *Literaturnoe obozrenie* 8 (1988): 48–54.

A lengthy review of *Doctor Zhivago*. Stresses the feelings of "happiness and liberation" as these readers' main reactions to this work. Finds it to be a novel not about the fate of the Russian intelligentsia per se but a "symbolist novel" dealing with myth.

Pomorska, Krystyna. "Doctor Živago." In *Themes and Variations in Pasternak's Poetics*, 74–90. Lisse: Peter de Ridder, 1975.

Demonstrates the new principles of composition used in *Doctor Zhivago*.

Reeve, F. D. "Doctor Zhivago." In *The Russian Novel*, 360–78. New York: McGraw-Hill, 1966.

Sendich, Munir, and Erika Greber. *Pasternak's Doctor Zhivago: An International Bibliography of Criticism (1957–1985)*. East Lansing, Mich.: Russian Language Journal, 1990.

The most complete bibliography of publications relating to *Doctor Zhivago* up to 1985. Includes all materials previously listed in Sendich's earlier bibliographies published in *Russian Language Journal* 30, no. 105 (1976): 109–52; *Russian Language Journal* 32, no. 113 (1978); and *Bulletin of Bibliography* 37, no. 3 (1980): 105–26.

Siniavskii, Andrei. "Nekotorye aspekty pozdnei prozy Pasternaka." In *Boris Pasternak and His Times*, 359–71. Berkeley and Los Angeles: Berkeley Slavic Specialties, 1989.

A nuanced defense of *Doctor Zhivago*'s "weaknesses" by one of Russia's greatest living authors.

Smirnov, Igor' P. "Dvoinoi roman (o 'Doktore Zhivago')" [A double novel (about *Doctor Zhivago*)]. *Wiener Slawistischer Almanach* 27 (1991): 119–36.

Argues that *Doctor Zhivago* hides beneath its surface a whole second novel, a cryptogram, that can help to decipher Pasternak's historical and philosophical views.

Vozdvizhenskii, Viacheslav. "Proza dukhovnogo opyta" [Prose of spiritual experience]. *Voprosy literatury* 9 (1988): 82–103.

Focuses on Pasternak's use of lyric device to create an epic.

Weststeijn, Willem G. "Metaphor and Simile in *Doktor Zivago*." *Essays in Poetics* 10, no. 2 (1985): 41–57.

Argues that Pasternak's novel must be judged in the light of the European modernist novel and not seen as a work of classical Russian realism.

Contributors

Carol J. Avins is Associate Professor of Slavic Languages and Literatures at Northwestern University.

Edith W. Clowes is Professor of Russian and Comparative Literature at Purdue University.

Jerome Spencer has an M.A. in Russian Language and Literature from Purdue University and is a law student at Georgetown University School of Law.

Boris Gasparov is Professor of Slavic Languages and Literatures at Columbia University.

Dina Magomedova is a Docent at the Russian Humanities University of Moscow and a Research Associate at the Institute of World Literatures, also in Moscow.